THE OTHER SIDE OF THE PACIFIC

Problems of Latin America

A.I.I.A. Countries Series

GENERAL EDITOR: DEREK WHITELOCK

THE OTHER SIDE OF THE PACIFIC

Problems of Latin America

GILBERT J. BUTLAND

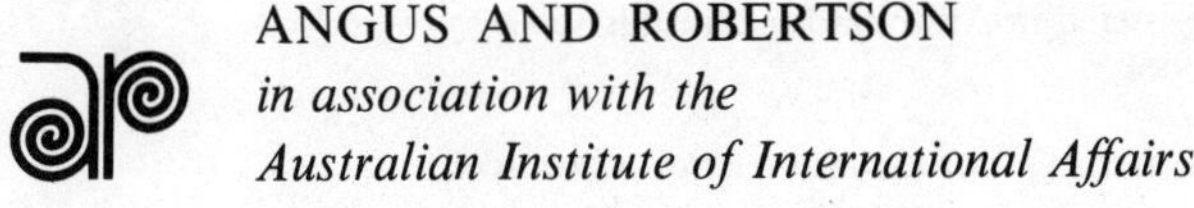

ANGUS AND ROBERTSON

in association with the

Australian Institute of International Affairs

First published in 1972 by
ANGUS AND ROBERTSON (PUBLISHERS) PTY LTD
102 Glover Street, Cremorne, Sydney
2 Fisher Street, London
107 Elizabeth Street, Melbourne
167 Queen Street, Brisbane
89 Anson Road, Singapore

Having as its object the scientific study of International questions, the Australian Institute of International Affairs, as such, does not express opinions or advocate policies. The views expressed in this book are therefore the author's own.

National Library of Australia card number & ISBN
Hard bound edition 0 207 12398 5
Paper bound edition 0 207 12475 2

Registered in Australia for transmission by post as a book.

PRINTED IN AUSTRALIA BY WATSON FERGUSON.

Foreword

This brief but cogent survey of Latin America is the first in the *Countries Series,* a series of similar studies of countries planned by the Research Committee of the Australian Institute of International Affairs and published by Angus and Robertson.

Each book in the series will be an authoritative, up-to-date and readable examination of the preoccupations and policies of a country or area. Australian comparisons or connections, where relevant, will be stressed.

Geoffrey Jukes' *The Soviet Union in Asia* will be published shortly by Angus and Robertson and titles for the series are being prepared on Canada, Japanese foreign policy, New Zealand, India Pakistan and Bangla Desh, Britain, China, Ceylon and Ireland.

The Institute is confident that the *Countries Series* will be of value to senior secondary and tertiary students and to all interested in international relations, a subject which is now of vital concern to us all.

DEREK WHITELOCK
April, 1972

Acknowledgments

The author is grateful for the permission of the Longman Group to reproduce some maps and diagrams from his book *Latin America: a Regional Geography*. Appreciation and gratitude is recorded of valuable editorial help provided by Dr Derek Whitelock, of cartographic help by Mrs Marion Schofield, and of secretarial help by Mrs Clarissa McGlynn.

Acknowledgment is also made of material from the *Statistical Abstracts of Latin America* compiled by the Latin American Center of the University of California at Los Angeles, which facilitated the construction of Figures 10 and 11 and the tables on pages 31 and 33.

The author is particularly indebted to analyses of current events provided by *Latin America,* a weekly political and economic report published by Latin American Newsletters Ltd., and edited by John Rettie, Christopher Roper, Hugh O'Shaughnessy and Jo Beresford.

Plate 8 is reproduced by kind permission of Lan Chile, and Plates 14 and 15 are from Associated Press Ltd. Other photographs have been provided by the author.

Contents

Illustrations

Preface

In the decade of the 1960s Australia began to take more interest in the countries on the other side of the Pacific. Trade Commissioners blazed the trail, and exhibitions of Australian products, new embassies in Rio de Janeiro, Buenos Aires, Santiago and Mexico City, and a significant increase in trade between the two continents were all evidence of a growing awareness of the potentialities of inter-continental contacts. In Australia, the establishment of Spanish language and literature courses and of Schools of Hispanic Studies in several universities, and the teaching of Spanish in some high schools were further indications of a realisation of the importance of the language spoken by 200 million Latin Americans and of their rich historical, literary and cultural endowment.

It is only in this decade that the advantages of air travel have been extended to direct services between the two continents, as previously travellers in either direction between Latin America and Australia were obliged to make connections in the United States. During the period of writing this book the Chilean air line, *Linea Aerea Nacional* (LAN), has thrust out from Santiago to Easter Island and thence to Tahiti, from where there are frequent services to Australia. This has provided the first possibility of a trans-South Pacific journey between the two continents. Previous to this, by means of Qantas' fiesta route, first established in 1964, the stop-over in Mexico City of many thousands of travellers facilitated the first real contact of large numbers of Australians with a Latin American land and culture previously unknown and ignored.

This awakening to Latin America is, of course, all to the good. Too often, in the past, a particularly magnificent or physically great achievement in Australia has been hailed as "the largest in the Southern hemisphere," in a facile assumption that if it were the largest in Australia, this automatically bestowed the wider claim, for, after all, the other two continents were largely undeveloped!

There is, of course, often much truth in such claims. In spite of its long history, large population and wealth of natural resources, Latin America is still lagging in development and beset with a complex web of problems, and it is opportune that some attempt should be made to disentangle the threads which give rise to its difficulties. It is hoped that this small volume may provide readers

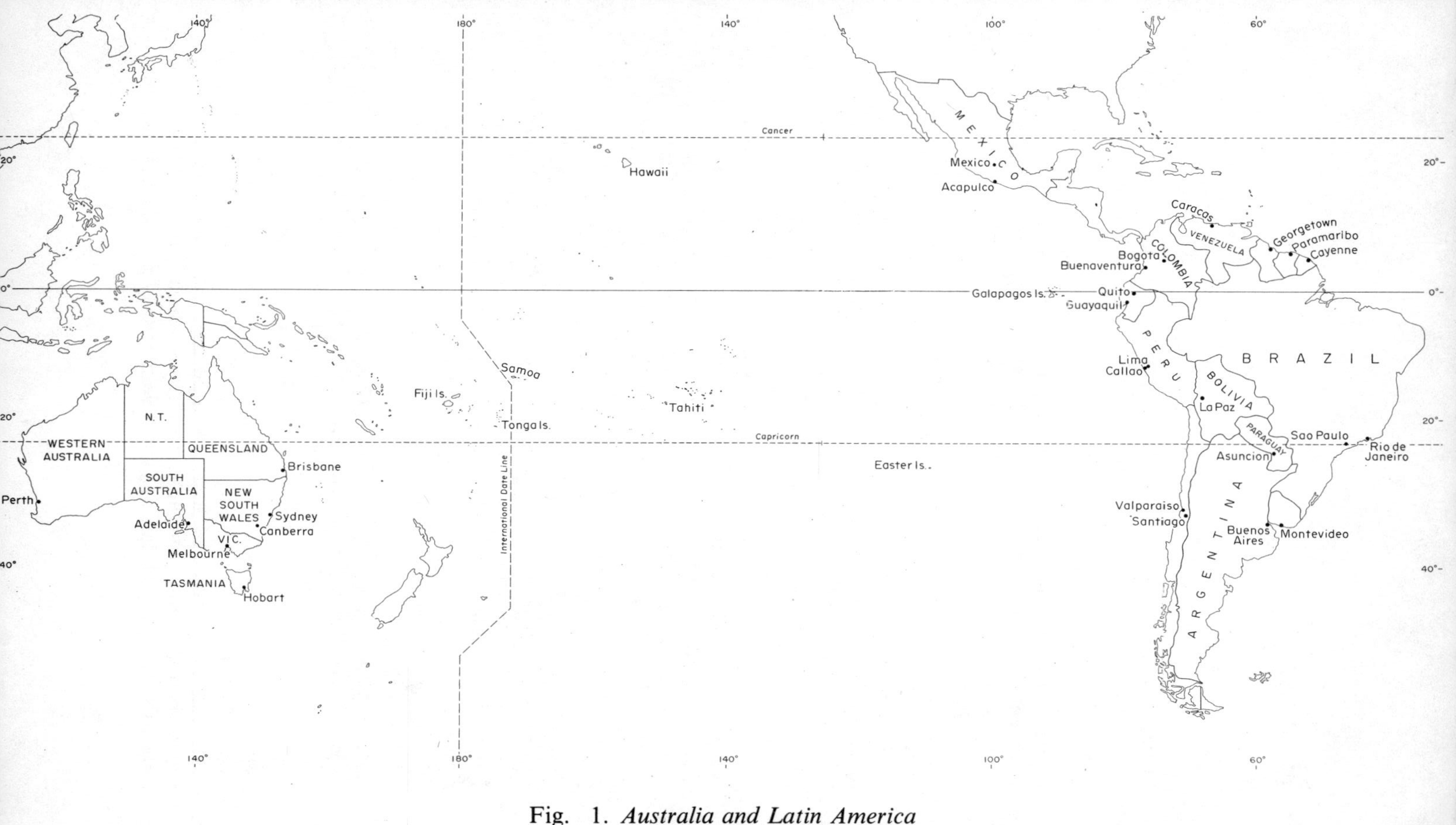

Fig. 1. *Australia and Latin America*

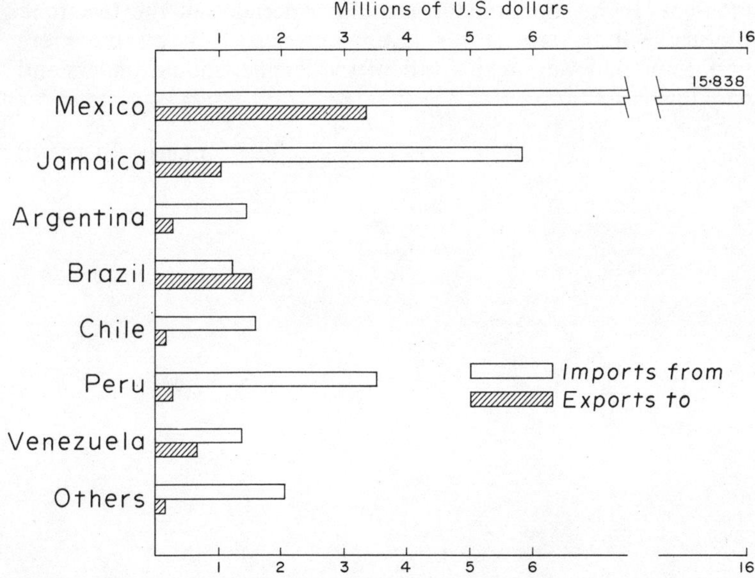

Fig. 2. *Australia's Trading Partners in Latin America*

in this continent with a starting point from which they may delve more deeply and sympathetically into the problems facing their distant neighbours across the lonely wastes of the Southern Pacific.

The canvas, however, is an enormous one. Boris Goldenberg has said that "no one can pretend to know all the essential facts about a big and heterogeneous area which is in a constant state of flux", and the more one sees of the lands and peoples of Latin America the more one's limitations are realised. The author spent five years of his life there, and has since visited at various periods most of the nations composing the continent. It is with this background of his experiences, supported by information and study of developments in a continent where data are not particularly easy to come by, that he presents this brief outline analysis.

Not all students of Latin America would agree with the assessments contained in the following pages. The weight of the factors involved in the problems discussed can be judged so variably that, inevitably, interpretations of their significance must differ. Few would deny, however, the intermeshed character of the problems entailed in the society, economy and politics of the Latin American area, and the author has tried to elucidate these as objectively as possible, stressing those he thinks are of greatest moment. In his opinion the last three decades of the twentieth century will be crucial for Latin America. It is all the more important that we, on this side of the Pacific, should understand why this is so.

GILBERT BUTLAND

I

If there is anything contradictory in the world, or a place where the most violent contrasts exist, that place is Latin America

GERMAN ARCINIEGAS

Introduction

Geographical differentiation: historical background: political fragmentation. The multi-variate contrasts: Haiti and Trinidad: Paraguay and Uruguay.

One of the greatest problems inherited by Latin America and Latin Americans is the name of the continent and its appendages, and the misinterpretations which arise from it elsewhere in the world. While, undoubtedly, a convenient title to designate all the lands south of the United States-Mexican border, it has led so many people to assume that there is a unity, a close similarity, an identity of interests, an expected pattern of common reactions, and even a susceptibility to the same kind of natural disasters, earthquakes, floods and hurricanes.

It is therefore not surprising that from the pens of those who should know much better, flow cliches and platitudes such as "typical Latin American reactions", "Latin American dictators" and "Latin American ebullience or siesta-like procrastination". All continents suffer to some extent from this tendency that the nations they contain "are lumped together", but none to the same extent as does Latin America. Every literate person recognises the gulf between the European countries of Albania and Holland, and between the Asian countries of Afghanistan and Israel, and few indentify Mexico as typically North American. Yet how many could even vaguely distinguish the gulf between Paraguay and Uruguay, geographically, historically, culturally, economically and politically?

Indeed, immediately an attempt is made to defend the omnibus title of Latin America, weaknesses in the defence become apparent as the many exceptions arise which qualify any set of generalisations made about the countries of the area.

It may be argued that the whole area has been exposed to a Latin culture, but what about Barbados, the Bahamas, Guyana and the considerable area of almost totally Indian population? The latter folk similarly prevent one generalising about Latin-derived ethnic or linguistic homogeneity. It sounds platitudinous to say the area is a continent of contrasts, but it is useless to attempt to understand Latin America without a realisation of the emphasis which must be placed on the multi-varied differentiation existing in the separate political units which compose it. Not only are there great contrasts in geography, in history, in cultures, and in politics, but these components do not fall into a nicely overlapping order and logical sequence derived one from the other. And the different segments themselves often stand out in sharp contradistinction within one country.

Had Símon Bolívar's dream of a united one-state South or Latin America ever evolved, there would still be most of these startling contrasts. Nevertheless, the political fragmentation of the continent into its present three dozen or so governmental units has done much to entrench old contrasts and to create others. Most students of Latin America today would agree that it is becoming increasingly difficult to write comprehensive volumes on Latin America which give any sense of a common structure, similar endowment or unified series of trends. The author once collaborated with a group of Latin American scholars in an effort to produce such a volume, and one of the principal reasons the attempt foundered was the necessity, at all stages and in every chapter, to qualify the statements in respect of this country or that region.

Political attempts like the Organisation of American States to polarise political unity; economic attempts, like the Latin American Free Trade Association (LAFTA) and the Central American Common Market (CACM), to coordinate trading policies; international attempts like those of the United Nations agencies to sort out the socio-economic difficulties of, and solutions for, the continent are all interesting examples of man's striving to use the common factors for the good of all, and indeed, often to weld strength from diversity. But the diversity exists in full measure, and this is where we must begin.

The physiographic complexity is the basic stage on which the drama is enacted (Fig. 3). The continent contains the world's greatest river basin, that of the Amazon, and the smaller but still extensive river plains of the Orinoco and the Paraná-Paraguay to

Fig. 3. *The Face of Latin America*

north and south of it. This vast area of some 2 million square miles of lowland, covered with apparently limitless areas of forest or grassland stands in sharp contrast to the great ranges of the Andes which tower over these plains on the west. Only the ranges of the Himalayas and Hindu Kush bear comparison with the Andes as a formidable and continuous barrier for over 4,000 miles, and nowhere else in the world outside the South Central Asian mountains do we find groups of peaks exceeding 15,000 feet in height. Nor are these precipitous elevations in reality limited to South America, for the transverse ridges of the Antillean mountains of the West Indies, running through Cuba, Jamaica, Haiti, the Dominican Republic and Puerto Rico, rise from abysmal ocean depths on both north and south. The 31,700 foot plunge from Puerto Rico's peak of El Yunque to the adjacent Brownson deep involves the greatest height-depth differential on earth.

Little wonder that the West Indies have endured many earthquakes and are as littered with volcanoes as are the snow-capped Andes, with exotic names like Chimborazo and Cotopaxi, and the great volcanic range which sweeps across south central Mexico, with Popacatepetl and Ixtaccuhatl. And in this latter area, man in this century saw the birth of a volcano Parícutin, which grew from a crack in a farmer's field to a sprawling peak 4,000 feet in height above the 7,000 foot high *meseta.*

But the mountains of Latin America are not all examples of very recent or current mountain building, for in the great Brazilian-Guianan plateau we have a 1½ million square mile fragment of a great super-continent of the Southern hemisphere, embracing most of Africa, the Deccan of India and much of Australia, stretching back into the dawn of geological history and endowed with vast mineral deposits from mines of diamonds to whole landscapes of iron ore. These elevated tableland surfaces characterise much of Brazil, Venezuela and the Guianas. They provide high monotonous landscapes similar to those of the great meseta-like basins of Mexico.

The variety of structural landscapes is reflected in the contrasts of coastal features which fringe them. They include the magnificent harbours of the Brazilian coast, such as that of Rio de Janeiro, which contrasts with the paucity of harbours on the mountain wall coast of the Pacific; and the mangrove enveloped deltas of the Amazon and Orinoco contrasting with the sparkling coral-fringed beaches of Jamaica and Barbados and the long strands of Uruguay.

The physiographic contrasts are, of course, not all dependent on structure and geology, but are equally important in respect of climate and vegetation. Latin America has some of the rainiest areas on earth and other areas where meteorologists have never recorded rain. Great deserts or semi-deserts sweep through the continent from southern Ecuador to southern Argentina. An unbroken mantle of forest covers Amazonia and much of the coastal areas of Middle America. In Argentina grasslands stretch out to an unbroken horizon as circular as that created by a pebble dropped in water. And there is every conceivable variety intermediate to these major types of desert, forest and grassland. The Brazilians try to classify them with such terms as *campo limpo, campo cerrado, caatinga* indicating the proportionate amounts of tree distribution and/or the types of scrub and forest characterising the landscapes. Nor are all the vegetational gradations associated only with areal spread but are altitudinally dependent on temperatures and rainfall from sea-level to over 20,000 feet, providing another bewildering variety of vegetational changes.

The physiographic mosaic has then had imposed upon it an historical occupation of some forty centuries which in many respects shows little conformity with the usually accepted pattern of human occupance on the most favoured lands. We find, therefore, citadels of community living high on the precipitous slopes of the Andes towering over the headstreams of the Amazon, like Macchu Pichu and Abiceo, the highest railways in the world thrown over yawning chasms of the Peruvian Andes, and the centres of the highest cultural achievement of pre-Hispanic America located on the dry scrub-covered limestone peninsula of Yucatán. On the other hand, vast expanses of interior Brazil are still largely untouched and are a paradoxical contradiction to the boulder-strewn arable patches scratched from precipitous mountain sides by the Andean Indians.

The historical occupance of the continent is a three-fold sequence—indigenous, European colonial, and modern—but the strength of the impact of these three cultures produces an historical mosaic as varied as the physiographic one. Some areas—Mexico City itself is a good example—have quite markedly experienced all three phases. Others, like the Gran Sabana plateau of Venezuela, have in reality experienced none, and are virgin wilderness. And there are the areas, like hundreds of Andean settlements, which have remained indigenous in occupance, or are fossilised colonial remnants like the city of Ouro Preto, or are brand new twentieth century creations like Brazil's steel centre of Volta Redonda. But, of course, the pattern generally is not so simple as that, for in most cases there is an amalgam of the three cultures in every variety of proportions.

Fig. 4. *The Colonial Conquest of Latin America*

Again, the sociological and economic implications of this variable historical occupance are proportionately varied, from the primitive Indian subsistence society and economy of much of Amazonia and scores of remote Andean settlements to the highly sophisticated, industrial and commercial societies of many of the capital cities and new urban centres.

Complicating these basic physiographic, historical and socio-economic mosaics is the political fragmentation of Latin America. Owing its origins predominantly to the colonial pattern of administration developed in the Spanish, Portuguese and other European colonies (Fig. 4), the partition of the continent into the thirty-eight separate political units now composing it has magnified rather than diminished the other contrasts contained within them. This is because in each unit different national policies have been brought into operation to transform, modify or affect the physiographic landscape, the historical inheritance and the socio-economic patterns composing the various nations. Varying degrees of nationalism, of attitudes to foreign investment, of adherence to democratic principles and of acceptance of change have influenced the present structure of the national units of Latin America. These have emphasised even more the complexity of contrasts which has been the theme of this introduction to the continent's contemporary problems.

It may be summarised and exemplified if we take two pairs of these political units which superficially, at least, appear to be, or should be, similar: a pair of West Indian islands, and a pair of Río Plata nations.

For this purpose Haiti and Trinidad epitomise most of the contrasts already mentioned (Fig. 5). Proportionately area for area and population for population they appear comparable demographically, as Trinidad has about one million population compared with Haiti's 5 million, but Haiti is more than five times as large as Trinidad. There, however, the resemblance ends and the physiographic, historical, socio-economic and political differences begin.

While there are some important areas of lowland in Haiti, the island for the most part is exceedingly mountainous, which is in fact the meaning of the indigenous word "Haiti". Large areas exceed 5,000 feet and there are peaks in excess of 10,000 feet. Trinidad, while in structural geology fundamentally similar, has as few areas of mountainous land as Haiti of lowland, and even the highest peaks top only 3,000 feet. The islands have similar climates, although, unlike Trinidad, Haiti lies in the path of hurricanes. Tropical crops like coffee, cocoa, sugar, bananas and

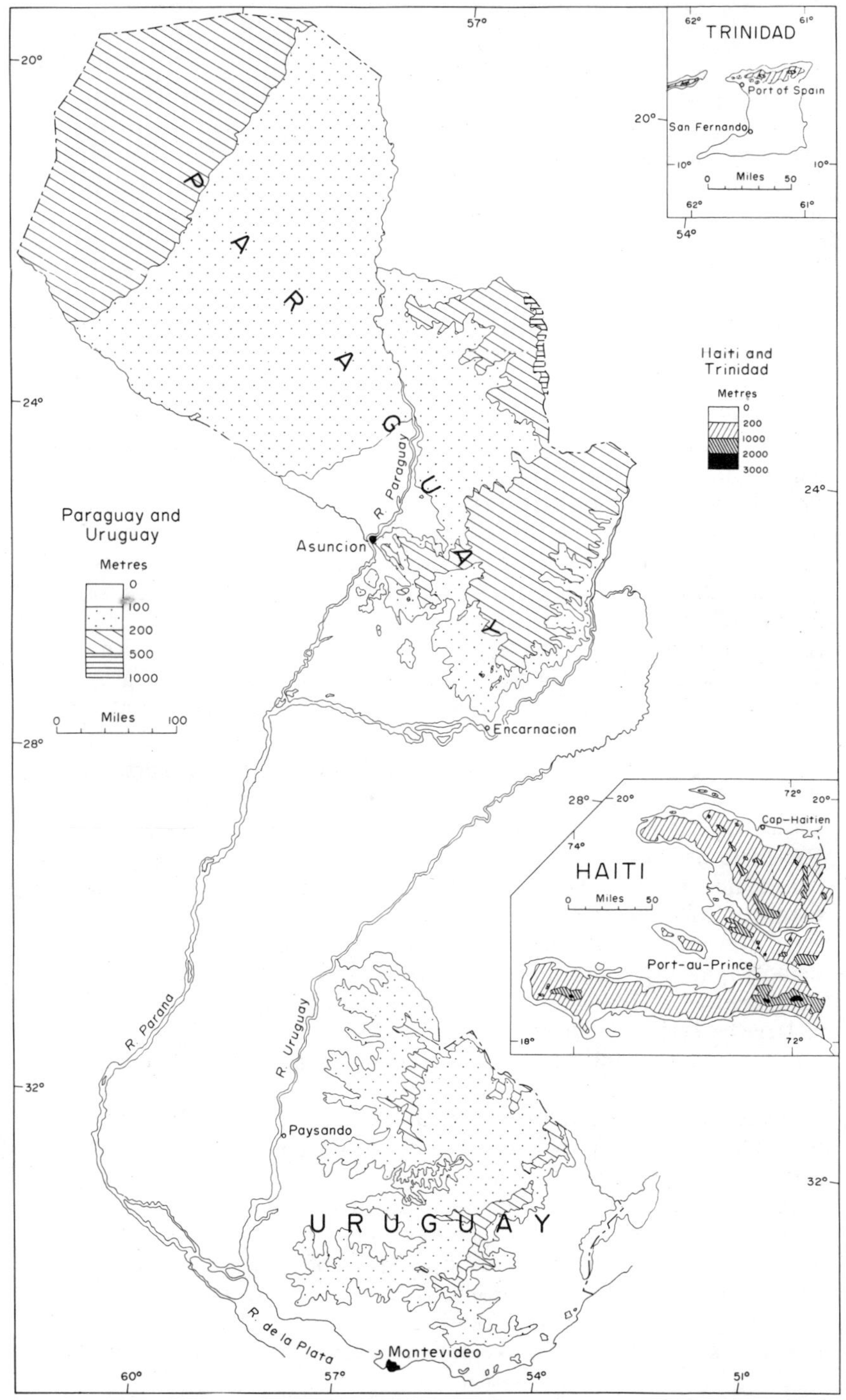

Fig. 5. *Latin American Contrasts. Haiti and Trinidad: Paraguay and Uruguay*

citrus grow well in both, but an exploitative peasant agriculture on mountainous terrain has impoverished Haiti's natural resources by a vicious sequence of deforestation, soil exhaustion and erosion so that production of subsistence crops is insufficient for the population, and of commercial crops is almost negligible. Yet in the eighteenth century it was one of the most productive agricultural colonies of any European nation, and certainly France's richest possession. Trinidad, on the other hand, after two and a half centuries of relative neglect by Spain, at the beginning of the nineteenth century entered a continuing era of agricultural expansion. Haiti, probably well endowed with a considerable variety of mineral wealth[1], has scarcely begun to explore or exploit this wealth. Trinidad, with only one major mineral inheritance, oil[2], has developed this resource to come within the first five petroleum producers in Latin America. The net result of the disparity in economic development is summarised in statistics such as these:

	Imports	Exports	National Revenue
Haiti	$ 36m	$ 36m	$ 28m
Trinidad	$783m	$730m	$257m

On the social and political fronts the disparities are equally great. Haiti is a homogeneous negroid state under one of the most ruthless dictatorships Latin America has ever known[3]; Trinidad with its multi-racial society, 42 per cent African in origin, 37 per cent Asian and 20 per cent of other groups is a stable democratically-run society[4]. Little wonder that 89 per cent of Haitians are illiterate compared with 11 per cent of Trinidadians, that Haiti's gross national product per capita is one-eighth of Trinidad's, and that Haiti has one doctor per 14,000 population, and Trinidad one for every 2,300.

A very similar contrast exists between Paraguay and Uruguay, the former a long established Spanish colony in the eastern interior of the continent, the latter a nineteenth century land of European immigrants on the north-eastern flank of the Plata estuary (Fig. 5). Ethnically, both are fairly homogeneous, Paraguay having a predominantly Indian *mestizo* population, Uruguay's

[1]Including at least 25 million tons of bauxite.

[2]And to a minor extent the asphalt of its unique pitch lake at La Brea.

[3]The death of François Duvalier in April 1971 has not changed this situation for the better. His son's government is spending more on the army and on the Tonton Macoutes (the dictator's secret police), and a new special military elite known as Les Leopards has been created.

[4]The disturbances in Trinidad in 1970 were atypical, had external connections, and, at the same time, were manifestations of discontent with endemic underemployment, a malaise common to all the West Indian islands.

population an Ibero-Italian foundation. Neither country appears to have any great mineral wealth, and their economic fortunes probably for all time will be dependent on agricultural-pastoral production. Yet Paraguay is, economically, a dependent colony of Argentina, Uruguay a stubbornly independent state always dissociating itself from any subservience to its great neighbours to the south and north. Paraguay has a perennial dictatorship; Uruguay, for long, has been the continent's most conspicuous example of a social democracy (despite the Tupumaros unrest of 1970-71). This explains why one-third of all Paraguayans live outside their country rather than within it, and why defence expenditure absorbs as much of the Paraguayan budget as education and health combined compared with Uruguay's three-fold devotion to these in relation to defence. It also explains why there are three times as many doctors, nurses and dentists in Uruguay, where illiteracy is one-third of the Paraguayan percentage.

Much of this contrast is the result of Paraguay's land-locked position (although other states in Africa and Europe have largely overcome this disadvantage), and still more the result of its fanatically militaristic history and self-imposed isolation. But whatever the cause, the contrasts between two superficially similar Latin American republics are dramatic and permanent for the forseeable future.

If there is still any doubt on this fundamental introductory premise of Latin American diversity, it may be removed by delving but a little into Costa Rican development and Nicaraguan under-development, Chile's industrialisation and Ecuador's lack of it, Argentine capitalist-type agriculture and Cuba's socialist transformation. Then, convinced that we are dealing with a continent of multiple variations, it is possible to take a look at some of the major problems besetting it in the last quarter of the twentieth century.

2

To redeem the Indian is to integrate the nation.

MEXICAN INDIAN INSTITUTE

Problems of Cultural Integration

The absence of racism: Brazil's multi-racial society: the two nations republic of Peru: Ecuador, Bolivia and Central America. The success of the Mexican Revolution.

When, in the first half of the sixteenth century, the Iberian conquerors overthrew the indigenous "empires" of the Incas, Aztecs and Mayas and asserted their sway over millions of Indians scattered throughout Latin America, the homogeneous ethnic composition of the continent was broken for all time. Not only did the Spanish and Portuguese administrators, soldiers, planters and mining prospectors interbreed with the Indian women to produce the predominant *mestizo* type of Latin American today, but the shortage of Indian labour in some parts, notably North-east Brazil, the West Indies and the Caribbean coastal lands, led to the importation of large numbers of African negro slaves. Intermixture of these with the Europeans and the Indians has produced other hybrids known as *mulattoes* and *zambos* (or *cafusos*) respectively. The nineteenth and twentieth centuries provided additional ethnic ingredients in the form of considerable European immigration principally into the southern areas of the continent. Almost all European nationalities were represented, but the Spanish, Portuguese, Italians, Germans and Poles provided the greatest numbers. To increase the complexity still further, about 2 million Japanese settled, principally in Brazil, in the 1920s and 1930s.

In spite of the great number of different racial contributions to the peopling of Latin America, there are some parts and some

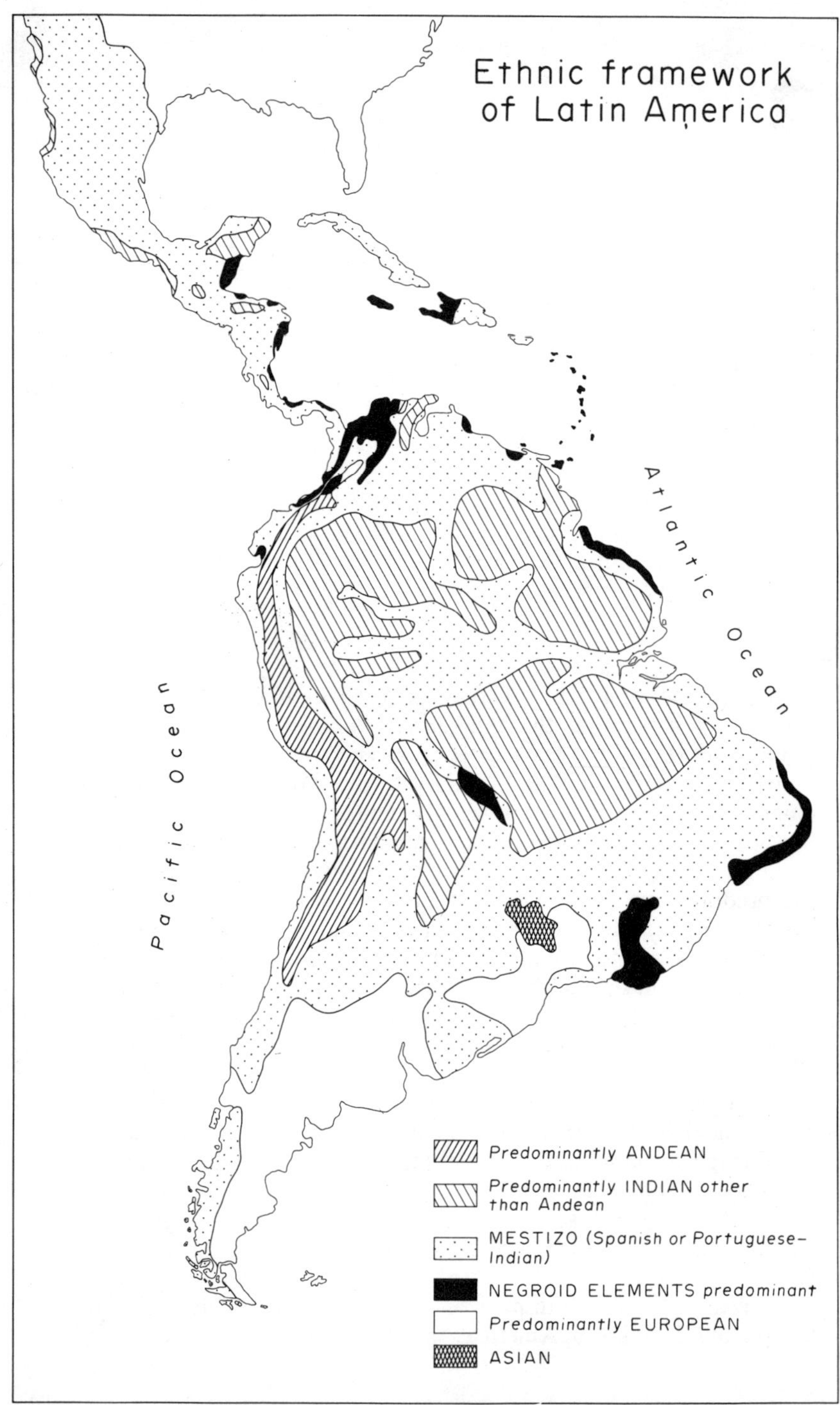

Fig. 6. *The Ethnic Framework of Latin America*

republics with a remarkably homogeneous ethnic make-up, and where problems of racial and/or cultural assimilation and integration scarcely exist (Fig. 6). Argentina and Uruguay fall into this category, as, in large measure, their 24 and 3 million populations respectively, are derived from the European immigrants who provided the labour force for the nineteenth century investment transforming their lands into the great meat and grain producing reservoirs of South America. There are historical differences between these pampa dwellers and the residents of the old areas of Argentina's North-west where Iberian colonists spilled over the Andes from Chile, but these are regional contrasts not dissimilar from those that exist in almost every nation. In a similar way the antipathies between town and country in Uruguay, between the metropolitan centre of Montevideo and the rural hinterland of the republic are little different from the clash of urban and rural populations of Sydney and the rest of New South Wales.

These are largely European homogeneities, but there are also examples of other racial cohesiveness. Haiti is overwhelmingly a negro republic with no minority problem of significance. Most of the small West Indian islands are similarly mulatto societies with no extraordinary racial or cultural cleavages. The mestizo republics of Chile, Colombia, Venezuela and Cuba, although differing in themselves in the degree of European-Indian mixture, have created homogeneous societies from a long inheritance of miscegenation, so that racial tension scarcely exists. Even where different national or cultural groups exist within them, such as the Germans of south-central Chile or the Antioqueños of the Medellín area of Colombia, the identification of these groups with Chile or Colombia, as the case may be, is so complete that no "problem" can be identified.

Indeed in terms of "race", problems in Latin America are few and the continent has, from its multi-racial inheritance, a tremendous advantage over some of the world's racially-tormented continents. No more conspicuous truth of this statement can be exemplified than in the case of Brazil. This vast nation of 96 million folk (1970) has its full share of Portuguese, Negroes, Italians, Japanese, Germans, Indians, Poles and every conceivable variety of mixtures of these and a host of other ethnic ingredients, so that one census in an effort to try to classify them asked those being enumerated to indicate which of the following skin colours they fell into:

(1) white	(4) dark	(7) mulatto and brown
(2) black	(5) Indian	(8) mameluco
(3) yellow	(6) mestizo	(9) cafuso (zambo)

It will be readily seen that under such conditions racial discrimination is rather difficult to practise. In fact most independent observers of the Brazilian scene would agree that few societies in the world, and none of a comparable size, exhibit so little racial tension or even friction. This does not mean to say that Brazil is a social Utopia, and there are problems of a class, occupational and cultural character, some of which are linked with the presence, absence of predominance of one or more racial or national groups. Some excellent detailed studies have been made of these problems[1], but the interesting consensus is that the tensions do not originate from race, nor are they associated exclusively with a particular ethnic group.

This racial harmony, characteristic of Latin America's largest and most populous state, is indeed the pattern for the continent as a whole. Only rarely has there been a display of violent antipathies between two opposing groups, the most notable occurrence being in British Guiana before independence. There, a population of some 800,000, almost equally divided between the descendants of negro slaves and the descendants of an immigrant Indian and Pakistani labour force, introduced in the last century to meet the shortage of agriculturalists following the emancipation of the slaves, clashed from a variety of economic, social and political causes. A population, no longer checked in its growth by the ravages of malaria, found its economic opportunities restricted by a monocultural sugar system and limited capital investment. The frustrations found expression in Dr Jagan's predominantly Indian-supported Marxist policies which frightened the United States that another Cuba might become entrenched in continental South America. In 1962 a part of the centre of Georgetown was burnt, and violence between the two communities became even more savage in 1964. Peace was restored by British troops, and a "fiddled constitution"[2] was imposed, which included a proportional representation system that was designed to restrict the opportunity of the Indian majority of achieving political dominance. As a result there has been a restoration of investment confidence and a greater promise of a long-delayed economic expansion.

The faster growth rate of the Indian part of the population means that it is bound to exert an increasingly predominant influence. In the meantime, it is to be hoped that a greater economic prosperity reflected in improved social conditions generally, and a

[1]See Bibliography.
[2]Harold Wilson's description.

Fig. 7. *The Culture Regions of Peru*

less exclusively racial base to the opposing political parties will restore communal peace. Similar communities coexist in nearby Trinidad, and with wise leadership, there is no reason why similar conditions should not obtain in Guyana.

The greatest problem, facing predominantly some of the Andean republics, is the relationship between the indigenous *Amerind*[1] peoples and the later immigrants and their descendants. It is particularly characteristic of Peru, and to a lesser extent of Ecuador, Bolivia and the Central American republics. The situation in Peru may be taken as an example of the constituents of the problem (Fig. 7).

Peru's population numbers are similar to those of Australia, approximately half the total being Amerind and the other half European and mestizo. The former are largely concentrated in the *Sierra*, the mountain and plateau Andean backbone of the country, and the slopes and forested plains of the Amazon and its headstreams included in eastern Peru. The European and mestizo people are, for the most part, the residents of the coastal cities, ports and irrigated valleys draining to the Pacific. A comparable distribution would be that if half the Australian population consisted of 6 million Europeans and mixed European/Aboriginal inhabitants occupying the coastal lands of Queensland, New South Wales and Victoria, and the other half of the population, 6 million Aborigines, occupying the tablelands and mountains from the Darling Downs to the Flinders Ranges.

The two Peruvian communities, however, are much more remote from each other. They are isolated by inhospitable and difficult terrain, by restricted communication links, and by the centuries of neglect of the Amerind people reflected in the poor provision of social services to them, so that they are an illiterate, ill-housed, inadequately fed and culturally deprived half of the nation.

When the *conquistador* Pizarro subdued the Inca Empire in 1531-3, he abandoned the Sierra as a major zone of colonial settlement and established Lima, "the city of the kings", in a coastal location. For three centuries it was the heart of imperial rule in the southern continent and the *Costa* became the zone of European settlement, of plantation agriculture, of industrial development and commercial investment. The Europeans were only interested in the Sierra for its mining wealth, for the extraction of which there was an abundant and cheap labour supply in the form of the Amerind population.

[1]The term coined to describe the indigenous American Indian peoples, as distinct from the Indian and Pakistani immigrants to Guyana and Trinidad.

There has, therefore, developed in Peru, a republic of two nations, of two cultures, separated racially, linguistically, socially and economically. Politically the Indian half of the republic scarcely exists and for millions the concept of a nation-state means nothing. Their existence in primitive hovels, scratching a subsistence living from a few patches of tilled land often separated from each other by miles of narrow tracks, chewing the coca leaf to assuage the pangs of hunger and struggling constantly merely to survive, contrasts starkly with the lives of the coastal Peruvians who control their destiny.

Just as the Aborigines in Australia were so long a forgotten fragment of the population, so the Amerind half of the Peruvian population was forgotten, and indeed almost unknown to the coastal Peruvians, except in so far as refugees from the harsh living conditions of the Sierra drifted into Lima, Callao and the other coastal cities seeking a better livelihood. The one individual mainly responsible for awakening the conscience of Peru towards its responsibilities to the Sierra Indians has been Haya de la Torre. His influence on Peruvian politics for half a century has been more marked than that of any other person, and governments have either had to work with his support or overtly and dictatorially suppress him and his followers. For over five years, from 1949 to 1954, he sought asylum in the Colombian Embassy in Lima. Had the results not been "cooked" he would have been President of Peru in 1931. His party did win the only contested elections of 1936, 1945 and 1962, but at all times military dictatorships ensured they did not gain power.

Obviously the cost of incorporating the Indians into the nation shocked the land-owning and other vested interests of Peru as much as did Haya de la Torre's socialist principles and programme that would have brought about the transformation. It is commendable however that the majority of the articulate (i.e. voting)[1] population of Peru do support the long overdue and massive effort needed to integrate the Amerinds into the nation. In the last democratic elections in 1963 Haya de la Torre was runner-up for the Presidency, and his party, the *Apristas (Alianza Popular Revolucionaria Americana)* constituted the largest single party in both the Senate and the Chamber of Deputies.

In a country in which politics had been hitherto "a contest among military leaders, rich landowners, and agents of foreign capital to see which group would gain the privilege of getting the

[1]The voters number only 2½ millions, as the franchise is based on literacy, which virtually eliminates most of the Sierra Indians.

graft and spoils of office",[1] the Aprista movement was the first attempt to create a political organisation that could find solutions to the problems that still confront Peru. Having its origins in the early 1920s, it was originally meant to be an organisation for all Latin America, but it made its greatest progress in the country of its origin, despite continued persecution and suppression of its activities.

While their philosophy in the course of half a century has evolved in response to fifty years of dynamic events in the continent and in the rest of the world, the principal trends have been somewhat xenophobic (especially in relation to the United States' domination of Latin America), agrarian and socialist.

These facets have evolved from the Aprista interpretation of history that the problems of Peru arise from the fact that ever since the arrival of the Spaniards two hostile cultures have been living side by side, and that only by merging the two could a road be opened to orderly development. This revaluation of the role of the Indian is central to Aprista philosophy and most of their other platform planks are derived from it, such as the unification of Indo-America, land reform, and cultural and economic emancipation. Throughout there has been a belief that the only secure basis on which their programme can be achieved is that of non-violent political activity and the presentation of their policy so that "the most illiterate and backward Indian is able to understand what the Aprista movement proposes to do."[2]

Dr Kantor, who has made a thorough study of Aprista ideology summarises it thus:

> The Apristas put the redemption of the Indian in the forefront of their program. They view the Indians as an alien body living alongside the rest of the Peruvian population, but not sharing the life of the country. Further they see the Indians as an oppressed class which must be freed if Peru is ever to progress because the Indians comprise the majority of the population. The problem is primarily economic and not one of race or color. They maintain that not all Indians are exploited and not all those exploited are Indians. . . . The root of the problem, according to the Apristas, is how to incorporate the Indian into the life of the country. They claim that if the Indian is kept uneducated and living in poverty and filth, he will never be able to contribute much to Peru. If the state intervenes to educate

[1]Kantor, Harry. *The Ideology and Program of the Peruvian Aprista Movement.* New York, 1966, p. 6.
[2]Ibid. p. 59.

him and improve his standard of living he will become a producer and a consumer and be able to contribute to the creation of a better Peru. The Apristas maintain they are not proposing such action because the Indian is Indian, but because the Indians form the exploited majority of the Peruvian population. Since the majority of the population is rural, they insist the problem resolves around the Indians' need for land.[1]

This Aprista drive for a social revolution to secure the incorporation of the indigenous people into meaningful participation in Peru's national life lost its direction in the 1960s. Whether by frustration or a sense of hopeless failure to achieve power in spite of popular support, the party drifted into an unnatural coalition with their most hated opponents, and the sense of revolutionary mission of *Aprismo* has probably disappeared permanently.

Fortunately the *Acción Popular* party, led by Belaúnde, and founded in 1956, seized the banner of cultural integration. This time, however, it was based less on a sweeping Indian socialistic take-over of Peru, but rather on a bridge between Coast and Sierra, whereby co-ordinated economic planning would secure the best results from the industrial and commercial enterprises of the Coast and from the communal landownership and labour of the indigenous folk of the Sierra. "Belaúnde envisioned a genuinely pluralistic country in which the coast could advance with its Westernised, capitalist traditions modified but not eradicated, while the Sierra progressed through its at least semi-socialistic Inca customs."[2]

The Acción Popular programme was based on Belaúnde's personal knowledge of the Andean communities, and the widespread support it received from nearly all sectors of articulate Peru resulted in the democratic election of Belaúnde to the Peruvian presidency in 1963. Despite congressional opposition and his overthrow by a military coup in 1968 (see pp. 80-82) his administration during its five years of office accomplished much and perhaps convinced the more politically aware Indians that at last there was a government genuinely concerned with their interests.

By agrarian reform measures and the redistribution of Andean lands; by the institution of governmental missions to the Indian communities to encourage cooperative programmes of road construction and the establishment of health clinics and schools; by

[1]Kantor, op. cit., pp. 84-5.

[2]Pike, Frederick B. "Peru" in Véliz, C. (ed.) *Latin America and the Caribbean: A Handbook*. London, 1968, pp. 93-4.

the creation of *Cooperación Popular*, a form of Peace Corps, the members of which shared their technical knowledge with the Indians to help them take their first steps into the twentieth century; Belaúnde did more to bridge the Costa-Sierra chasm than all his predecessors combined.

Nor is it to be assumed that his overthrow by the military means an end of the programmes he introduced, for the 1968 Revolution was not one of reactionary generals acting on behalf of the oligarchy for the status quo, as has been the customary pattern of military intervention. Instead it was a revolution of a younger group of nationalists, characteristic of a new force in Latin American politics, concerned with social progress, the economic interests of Peru and its emancipation from foreign imperialism. Indeed it was with their support that Belaúnde had carried forward his policies of road building and integrated community development. Just as Perón identified his regime with the *descamisados* of Argentina's urban proletariat, it is not impossible that the Velasco Alvarado regime may do much to weld a Peruvian nation from its disparate halves.

As already indicated, one of the principal economic means by which the Sierra population can solve its problems is agrarian reform, and since 1962 much has been achieved. Not only have large and inadequately used estates been broken up, but there have been steps towards land amalgamation, for *minifundia* or land fragmentation is almost as great a problem as *latifundia*, the system of vast properties. Changes in land tenure, however, are by no means the single answer to agrarian poverty and finance. Improved agricultural methods and training in management practices are usually more important.

The magnitude of this task, plus the overcoming of malnutrition, disease, illiteracy and apathy, is so great, however, that even if a warlike operation were mounted now it is difficult to see how this problem of cultural integration could be overcome in this century. Many people, overwhelmed by the size of the problem find a refuge in declaring it to be insurmountable because of the apathy, lack of self-help and ignorance of the masses concerned. Certainly it is often difficult to know where to begin, as the problem has so many facets. Perhaps above all is the need to reduce the pressure of population on inadequate land resources by moving many of the 6 million inhabitants of the Sierra into the largely unpopulated eastern half of Peru.

One of Belaúnde's high priorities in his programme was the *carretera marginal de la selva*, the forest highway, along the eastern slopes of the Andes to link the interior lands of Peru with those of

Ecuador and Bolivia, and to encourage colonising movements of these Sierra Indians into Peruvian Amazonia, but this is easier said than done and some aspects of this demographic problem will be discussed in a later chapter (Fig. 13). The problem is similar, although by no means identical, in Ecuador. There the capital of the Spanish colony was located in the Indian heartland at Quito. Although the economic, social and political problems of the Indian inhabitants are not greatly different, the terrain of many of the Ecuadorean mountain basins is more favourable, and the Indians are less isolated and less remote from the currents of national life. In this century, however, the growth of Guayaquil (750,000) has so overtaken that of Quito (500,000) the capital, that inevitably the commercial interests of the coastal region tend to take priority over the solution of the problems of the Sierra.

Bolivia, where the Indians for centuries held a similar inferior status to the small minority of Europeans and mestizos, has, dramatically, in the last twenty years, done a great deal to incorporate the indigenous people into the nation. In 1952 the literacy test for the franchise was abolished and a vigorous agrarian reform and internal colonisation programme has been undertaken.

What had started as just another of the scores of Bolivian political revolutions became a great Indian resurgence. The indigenous people themselves put an end to the old social order by invading the great estates and demanding their rights as citizens. Fortunately the government of Paz Estenssoro, realising the value of incorporating the Indians, economically and culturally, into the Bolivia of the future, guided the social revolution wisely and, perhaps rather amazingly, secured the economic cooperation of the United States in the task, so that "Bolivia is at present in the process of becoming an Indian nation, or a modern nation that is predominantly Indian in culture."[1]

The position in respect of the Central American republics is less easy to define. Ethnically the Amerinds are in a clear majority in all the states making up the area, but economic and administrative power remains in the hands of the Europeans and mestizos. Although there are continuous areas of Indian occupance and in parts more isolated enclaves of indigenous folk in the midst of largely mestizo populations, basically the Indians are an exploited population of peasants and labourers. They are found mostly in the rural and small-town sectors or lower class of the larger urban centres. Central American governments often regard their Amerind populations as problems inhibiting development but in reality "the shoe is on the other foot" as the governments have done little

[1]John F. Goins, 1960.

to incorporate them economically and politically into the mainstream of the republic's life. A notable exception was that of the Guatemalan government of 1944-54 which was strangled by United States-aided intervention. Among the more hopeful aspects are the considerable efforts by some political parties, welfare organisations, and by the Peace Corps to mitigate the worst effects of the socio-economic repression. It is not easy to do this, however, for the Central American Indian, for the most part, retains his defensive posture of emphasising the "different" character of his race, culture and society.

The most successful achievement in eliminating this European-Amerind dichotomy is undoubtedly that carried out in Mexico. Unlike Peru, the colonial capital in Mexico was established on the site of the indigenous capital, and it has grown to be not only the largest city in Latin America but the centre of a great industrial and agricultural belt and indeed of the whole nation. Nevertheless by the end of the nineteenth century the concentration of agrarian power in the hands of the European and mestizo minority was more complete than that of most of Latin America. The fragmentation of the Indian majority into thirty-one major language groups and another twenty-one minor linguistic divisions presented a problem in this respect infinitely greater than that of the Indians of Peru who all speak Aymará or Quechua. In addition the pressure of population on poor land resources, illiteracy and malnutrition presented the Mexicans with a socio-economic problem of enormous proportions.

Identifying Indian ownership of land with the reconquest of liberty, the Mexican Revolution of 1911-21 set in motion a great national movement to consolidate the people into a wholesome Mexican nationality. The occupation of the great European and mestizo owned estates by the Indians was a material demonstration of the end of four centuries of alien domination, but the explosion of the predominantly Indian inheritance of Mexico found expression just as much in the great cultural renaissance exemplified by the paintings of Rivera, Orozco and Siqueiros all of which stressed the continuity of Mexico's Indian past. A comprehensive example of this Indian rebirth is the magnificent National Museum of Anthropology in Mexico City which displays the history, life and art of the indigenous peoples to thousands of Mexicans and visitors daily. "Not Cortés the Conquistador but Cuauhtémoc, his victim and the last of the Aztec princes, became the symbol of the nation".[1]

[1]Clissold, Stephen. "The Indian Heritage" in Véliz, C. (ed.) *Latin America and the Caribbean: A Handbook,* London, 1968, p. 755.

Although there is still an enormous task ahead to provide the rural Indian of Mexico with a decent standard of living in terms of an adequate and balanced diet and the benefits of educational and social welfare, the transformation of two parallel societies into one nation is so complete that it must be regarded as one of the great sociological achievements of the twentieth century. It has created for Mexico a period of political stability, of cultural independence, of national self-esteem and of economic growth, that is the envy of many other Latin Americans endeavouring to achieve the same goals in their own countries.

A particularly encouraging aspect of cultural integration in Mexico is that there is no regressive escape into a nostalgic introvert past. Instead there is a forward moving society becoming increasingly urban and industrialised and thereby overlain with many of the trappings of Western European or North American civilisation, yet Amerind in its foundations and basic structure, giving a national and homogeneous individuality to the whole Mexican nation and to the 50 million Mexicans who compose it.

3

Paradoxically, in the face of rapid urbanisation, Latin America continues to be a rural continent with its population sparsely distributed in large areas with every now and then a big metropolis.

CARMEN MIRÓ

Population Problems

Total population growth: problems of mal-distribution: mushrooming urbanisation on a colonial urban pattern: rural over-population: the undeveloped frontier: acute problem areas.

It is, of course, almost impossible to separate many of the problems of cultural integration from those associated with demographic pressures of one kind or another. It is now customary to talk about the Latin American population explosion, because there is increasing awareness that population growth in Latin America is proceeding at a pace faster than that of any other continent or major land region in the world. A profusion of statistics can indicate this. In 1900 its 63 million people represented 2.7 per cent of the world's population. Its present population of 300 million is about 8 per cent of the world's population, and present trends indicate that by the end of the century, with about 600 million (for Latin America's population now doubles every 23 years), it will represent 10 per cent of the world's population, and only Europe, India and China will have more people (Fig. 10).

This high growth rate is largely the result of high birth rates being maintained simultaneously with dramatic decreases in death rates (Fig. 11). In most republics in the last twenty years death rates have been slashed from 20 per 1000 to half that figure, largely as a direct result of improved health measures and the elimination of parasitic diseases such as malaria. If continued improvement in nutritional standards takes place and infant deaths are further reduced, and birth rates continue to be maintained, the growth rates will accelerate rather than decrease.

Fig. 8. *Population Distribution*

Yet, in spite of this rate of growth and absolute increase in numbers, Latin Americans are quick to point out that theirs is not a thickly populated continent. It contains 14 per cent of the world's land surface but only 8 per cent of the world's people, and this means an average population density of less than 40 per square mile. It will also be stressed that there are vast, relatively empty areas that are capable of economic occupation. So, apart from problems related to food production and the whole socio-economic framework of many parts of the continent, the major demographic problems facing Latin America are those related to population distribution (Fig. 8).

Before discussing these, however, it is important once again to stress that even the rate of population growth is a continental generalisation which conceals wide variations between the republics contained within it. Growth rates are three times as high in Costa Rica and Venezuela as they are in Uruguay and Bolivia. In the forty years since 1930, Argentina's population has doubled from 12 million to 24 million but in the same period Mexico's has tripled from 16 million to 50 million. In 1920 Ecuador's population of $1\frac{1}{2}$ million was similar to that of Uruguay. Today Ecuador's total exceeds 6 million and Uruguay's less than half that figure. These variations are almost entirely the result of differences in birth rates, for reductions in death rates have been continent-wide in their incidence. Birth rates in Mexico, the Central American republics, Ecuador and Venezuela are among the world's highest, whereas those of Uruguay and Argentina are comparable with those of Australia, the United States and Canada (Fig. 9).

The problems of population distribution that are most acute in Latin America are all related to rural over-population, mushrooming urbanisation and the difficulties facing attempts to colonise empty areas of the continent. Many of the areas of long occupation, whether indigenous, colonial, or both, are by any criteria, over-populated. While improved farming techniques, more intensive cultivation, agrarian reform and decentralised industrialisation could obviously provide more employment in most rural areas, the pressure of population on limited, indeed completely inadequate, land resources is so acute that the net result can only be underemployment, malnutrition, housing squalor, poverty and a host of associated deficiencies. Mention has already been made of the 5 million rural Haitians trying to wring a livelihood from an eroded mountain landscape, and of the Peruvian peon trudging miles between his miniscule plots in the high Sierra. But in most of the Andean republics and Middle American highland states, countless examples could be quoted of

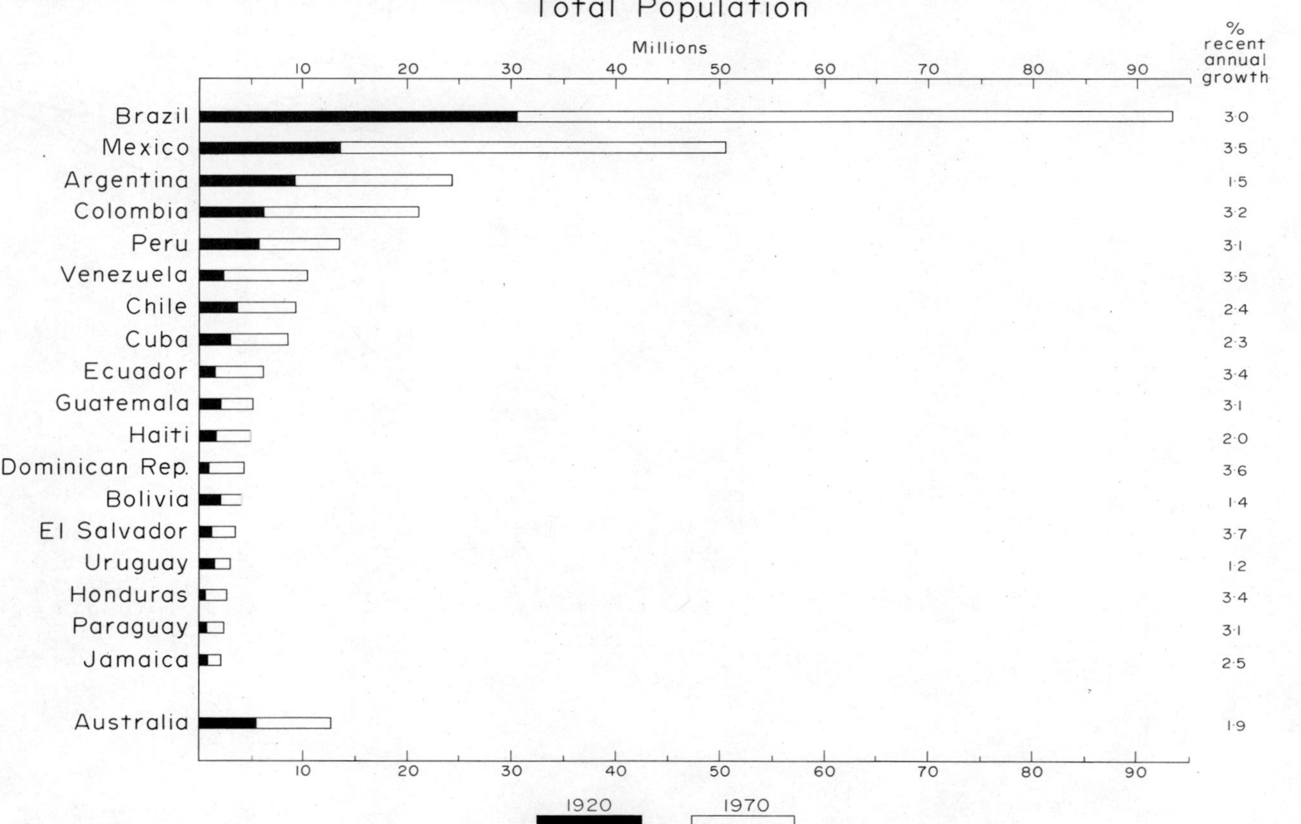

Fig. 9. *The Growth of Population*

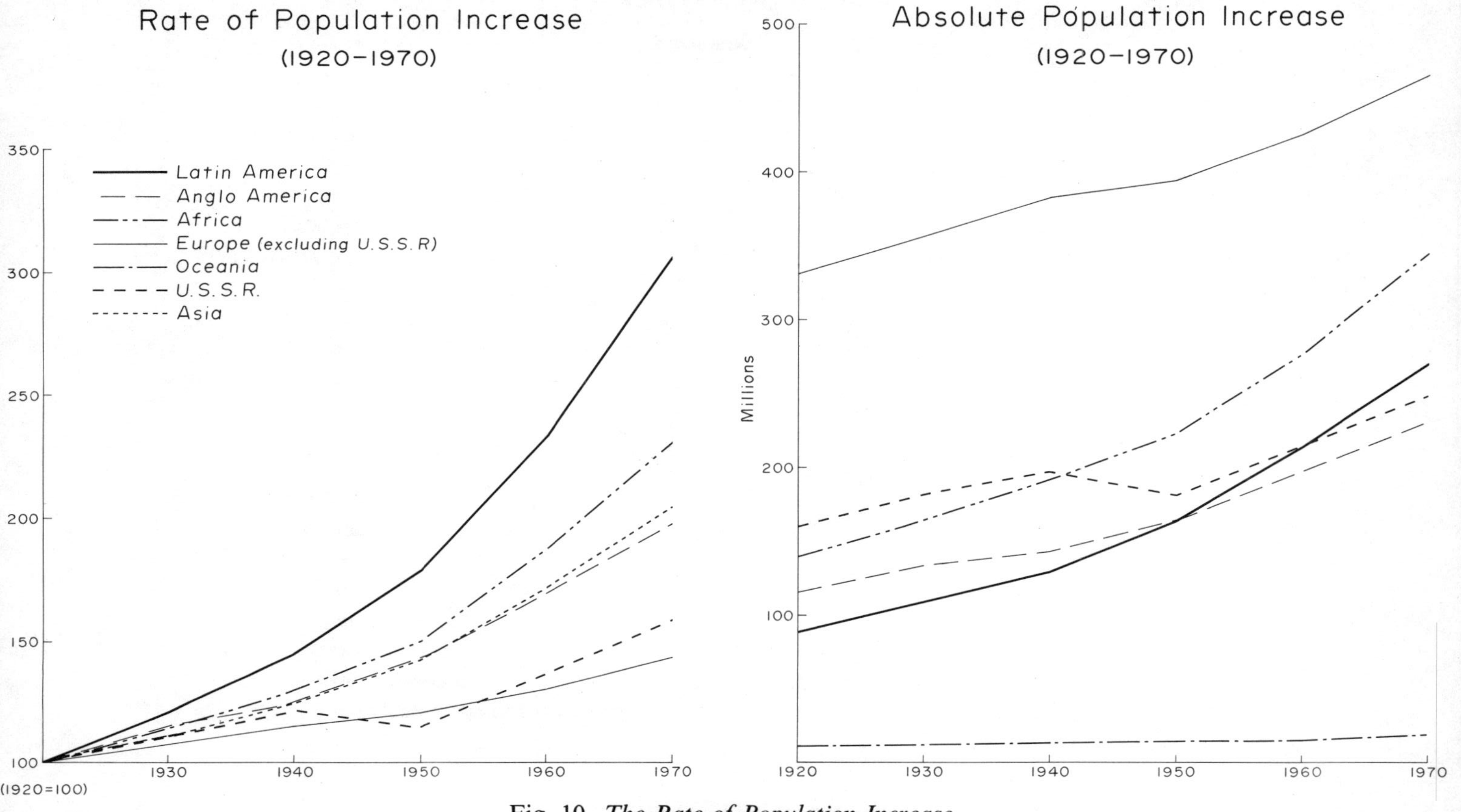

Fig. 10. *The Rate of Population Increase*

the pathetic attempts to cultivate precipitous slopes and the great expenditure of human energy merely to exist. When drought and flood also afflict these over-populated areas the consequences are obvious. One region, North-eastern Brazil, often scourged by both these natural disasters, and with a population exceeding 30 million, is the continent's greatest single area of endemic rural over-population.

The origin of this problem is, of course, long historical occupance associated with both the indigenous and the colonial avoidance of forested lands, but the demographic trends already mentioned, of falling death rates and maintained high birth rates, are exacerbating the problem to a bursting point.

The principal "relief" to the problem so far, has been a continuing rural-urban migration, which is characteristic of every political unit in Latin America to a greater or lesser degree. In the last twenty years the rural percentage of the population of Brazil has fallen from 64 per cent to 47 per cent of the total population; that of Chile from 41 per cent to 27 per cent, of

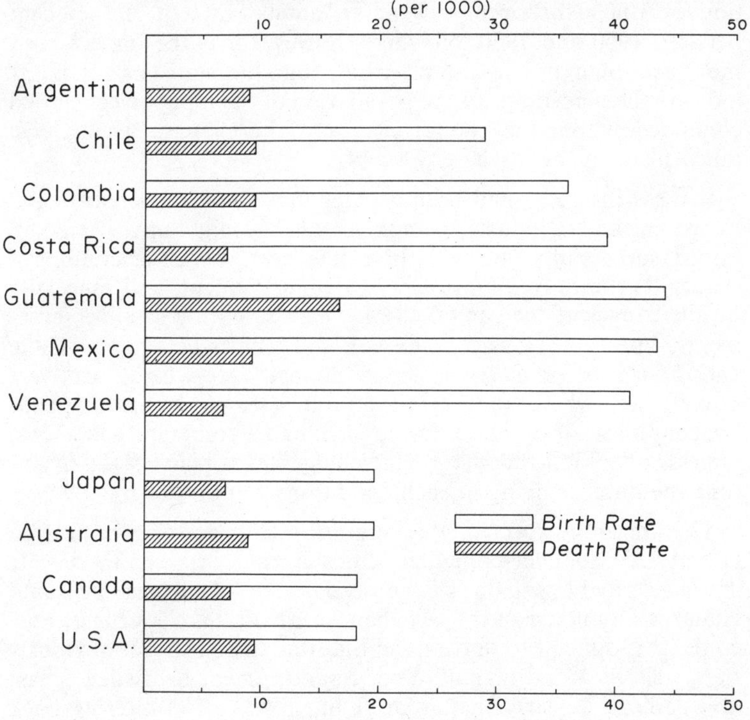

Fig. 11. *Selected Birth and Death Rates, 1967*

Colombia from 72 per cent to 55 per cent, of Peru from 61 per cent to 47 per cent. However it must be remembered that in every case the *relative* decline in rural population has not meant any *absolute* decline in numbers. In fact, population growth in rural areas has usually resulted in an increase of rural population despite the steady out-migration. Since 1950, in Brazil, rural population has increased by 11 million, in Peru and Colombia by 1.7 million each and even in Ecuador by over one million. In this respect the rural-urban flow in Latin America differs considerably from the Australian pattern where in most cases rural populations have declined both relatively *and* absolutely.

On the other hand, the increased urbanisation of the continent's population is the greatest single change in demographic distributions in Latin America. As a result of population growth and of the drift to the cities, since 1950, Brazil's urban population has rocketed from 19 to 50 million, Argentina's from 11 to 18 million, Chile's, Colombia's and Peru's 3 million each to 7, 8 and 7 million respectively. In Chile and Ecuador towns of a population of 10,000 or over grew at an annual rate of 12 per cent between 1950 and 1960. Nowhere, however, has the impact been more felt than in the capital cities, and the statistics on p. 31 indicate the percentage of the population of the republic concerned contained within the capital city, and the changes which have taken place in the last ninety years.

If these increases had been accompanied by a rapid expansion in housing and in industrial employment they might have been contained successfully. Instead there has been a vast accretion of shanty dwellings in almost every urban settlement, and especially on the fringes of the capital cities. These squatting satellite settlements, known variously as *favelas* in Brazil, *callampas* in Chile and *barriadas* or *villas miserias* almost everywhere, are vast poverty belts where some 30 million folk attempt to exist in appalling conditions of squalid housing, lacking all community facilities. Unless some radical demographic change takes place in the meantime the number living in such conditions will double by 1990.

The amazing aspect of this migration from an over-populated countryside to over-populated cities is that in general, despite the indescribable squalor of the favelas, the lot of these peasants is marginally better in the city than in the rural areas whence they come. It is difficult to understand that this can be so, yet obviously the persistency and magnitude of the movement over such a vast area indicates clearly that, were it otherwise, news filtering back from the city would check the rural exodus.

GROWTH OF CAPITAL CITIES

Country	Capital City (urban area)	Population 1970 (millions)	Percentage of Population in City 1880	1905	1930	1960	1970
BRAZIL	Rio de Janeiro*	4.03	3	4	4	7	8
MEXICO	Mexico City	3.35	3	3	5	15	15
ARGENTINA	Buenos Aires	7.0	12	20	20	32	31
COLOMBIA	Bogotá	2.06	1	2	2	8	11
PERU	Lima	1.83	3	3	5	19	21
VENEZUELA	Caracas	1.76	3	4	7	18	19
CHILE	Santiago	2.31	6	10	13	22	26
CUBA	Havana	1.54	13	15	15	18	22
ECUADOR	Quito†	.40	7	5	5	7	10
GUATEMALA	Guatemala City	.58	4	5	5	10	12
HAITI	Port-au-Prince	.24	1	4	4	5	7
DOMINICAN REP.	Santo Domingo	.58	1	2	3	12	15
BOLIVIA	La Paz	.36	3	4	5	10	11
EL SALVADOR	San Salvador	.32	4	5	8	9	11
URUGUAY	Montevideo	1.16	12	30	28	31	38
HONDURAS	Tegucigalpa	.17	3	4	4	5	8
PARAGUAY	Asunción	.31	3	12	14	18	20
JAMAICA	Kingston	.38	—	—	—	23	24

*Largest city São Paulo 5.4. †Largest city Guayaquil .65.

The attempts to cope with this vast additional immigrant population, especially in the capital cities, vary considerably from country to country. Large apartment blocks have been constructed on the site of some of the worst slum areas of Caracas. Similar rehousing has been carried out in Rio de Janeiro, followed by the burning and destruction of the shanty towns whose occupants have been rehoused. Undoubtedly the most successful attack on the problem has been in Puerto Rico, where hundreds of three-storey apartment blocks and thousands of simple three- and four-room bungalows cover vast acreages on the fringes of San Juan and other cities. All these measures in most countries are really only palliatives as they rarely equal the rate of growth of the squatters' settlements. Moreover, all countries, burdened with other demands of a gigantic dimension, such as the attempt to provide enough schools and hospitals for a galloping population increase, simply have insufficient funds to meet the housing shortage. An estimated one million additional hospital beds are needed just to satisfy the minimum reduced care of patients suffering from acute diseases. To meet all Latin America's housing requirements, involving the construction of at least 18 million new housing units, would require capital expenditure of at least 25 thousand million Australian dollars, or a third of the continent's total annual gross national product.[1]

Housing conditions in rural areas for the majority of the poor are similar to those they occupy in the cities, except perhaps in respect of the benefit of less congestion. In most cases, however, there is no electricity or sewerage, nor even outside sanitary facilities. A thatched roofed one-room cottage with a door and a window serves as home to over ten persons in the countryside and is considered a luxury.

These over-populated conditions, both in cities and in rural areas are exacerbated by the slow economic growth of Latin America in both agricultural and industrial sectors, as a result of which there is totally inadequate employment opportunity in town and country.

There has always been an important urban component in Latin American settlement since the dawn of the colonial occupation. Spaniards and Portuguese founded towns throughout their empires, and most capital cities date their origins to the first half of the sixteenth century, for example:

Panamá City	1519	Asunción	1537
Mexico City	1521	Bogotá	1538
Quito	1534	Sucre	1538
Lima	1535	Santiago	1541

There was thus a very early impetus to the growth of the metropolitan centres, and the recent stampede of population from rural areas to them has further accentuated their top-heavy character in population distribution in all the Latin American states. Thus a common pattern is of a capital with a population exceeding at least one million inhabitants, and no other urban centre remotely comparable with it in size as illustrated by the first four examples in the table on p. 33. Note also that this lop-sided pattern of urban centres is just as strongly entrenched in the smaller republics.

Mexico and Brazil each have other cities besides their capitals with populations exceeding a million, and each has at least a score of other cities with populations exceeding 100,000 and Colombia has a dozen cities of similar size.

[1]*Statistical Abstract of Latin America, 1967*. Latin American Center U.C.L.A., 1969.

Country	*Capital City*	*Population*[1]	*Next largest urban centre*	*Population*
Uruguay	Montevideo	1.2m	Paysandu	.06m
Peru	Lima	1.5m	Callao	.16m
Chile	Santiago	2.3m	Valparaíso	.28m
Argentina	Buenos Aires	7.0m	Rosario	.68m
Costa Rica	San José	340,000	Alajuela	20,000
El Salvador	San Salvador	281,000	Santa Ana	73,000
Guatemala	Guatemala City	577,000	Quetzaltenango	45,000
Honduras	Tegucigalpa	170,000	San Pedro Sula	59,000
Nicaragua	Managua	262,000	Leon	45,000
Panamá	Panamá City	343,000	Colón	60,000
Dominican Republic	Santo Domingo	561,000	Santiago de los Caballeros	86,000
Haiti	Port-au-Prince	240,000	Cap Haitien	24,000
Bolivia	La Paz	360,000	Cochabamba	95,000
Paraguay	Asunción	305,000	Encarnación	19,000

[1]The urban agglomeration.

The greatest socio-economic rift between metropolis and country occurs where the disparity is greatest and Montevideo's hegemony in Uruguay wins pride of place in this connection. Fitzgibbon[1] has made a fascinating study of the frictions which exist between the Uruguayan rural and city dwellers. The disparity is no greater than that of Sydney's share of New South Wales' population or Adelaide's of South Australia; and rural dwellers particularly in those two states will scarcely need an explanation of the problems facing them in respect of the concentration of population, capital investment, political interest and the services needed in the great metropolitan centres.

The paradox, of course, is that although there is such urban concentration in Latin America, the rural landscape generally is over-populated relative to the land resources available. This is chiefly because the distribution of population is so badly adjusted to the economics of the terrain. Tens of thousands of folk eke out an existence from subsistence agriculture and/or pastoralism on precipitous Andean slopes, boulder strewn and subject to the worst ravages of soil erosion, while millions of acres of the "interior" lands of Latin America are virtually uninhabited. The relatively empty eastern halves of nations like Bolivia, Peru, and Colombia stand in sharp contrast to the largely over-populated mountainous western halves. The crowded basins of central Mexico overlook the scantily-populated tropical plains and basins

[1]Fitzgibbon, R. H. *Uruguay, Portrait of a Democracy*. London, 1956, pp. 106-121.

of southern Mexico. The millions of the drought- and flood-affected North-east of Brazil have lived for centuries in ignorance of the uninhabited rolling plateaux of south and central Brazil. The congested islands of the Greater Antilles, contrasted with the largely untouched Guianan lands, form yet another facet of this general picture of mal-distribution of population.

In theory it would appear to be a relatively simple problem to solve. With modern technologies of road construction, land clearance and agricultural mechanisation, what could be simpler than moving populations from overcrowded regions to adjacent areas previously undeveloped? The redistribution would, of course, involve a vast financial investment for the states concerned, but an obstacle almost as important is the reluctance of the people to move. For generations they and their ancestors have built their pattern of living, their diet, their homes, their community structure on terrain, climate, vegetation, crops and animals associated with and indigenous to their highland environment. To make the change to an environment totally different in the tropical lowlands, often away from relatives and friends, to learn new methods and adapt their long-established mores to a new and strange land rarely proves an attractive proposition. When one considers how frequently immigrants to Australia from the United Kingdom return to their homeland, the Latin American phenomenon is not difficult to understand. The immigrants to Australia are literate and are moving, in most cases, from an urban culture to one not dissimilar "down under". Yet thousands annually return to their "Coronation Streets" in an almost vestigial nostalgia. The movement from western to eastern Bolivia is a much greater challenge from every point of view, especially to the largely illiterate peasant whose horizons for centuries have been the village of his birth and perhaps occasionally the market-town distant three or four hours walk over the hills.

Perhaps instead we should gaze in wonder and admiration at what has been achieved, at the road and rail construction linking Bolivia with Brazil (Fig. 12) providing an artery of settlement of the lowlands east of Cochabamba, at the 100,000 settled there since 1953, at the gigantic concept of the Andean Marginal Highway in Peru linking the settlements which have been pushed into the so-called *ceja de montaña* (literally "the jungle's eye-brows"), at the integrated development schemes of Mexico's South in the Papaloapán and Balsas basins, whereby flood control measures, transport networks, power provision and agricultural technology have provided new homelands for folk from the crowded basins of the plateau (Fig. 13).

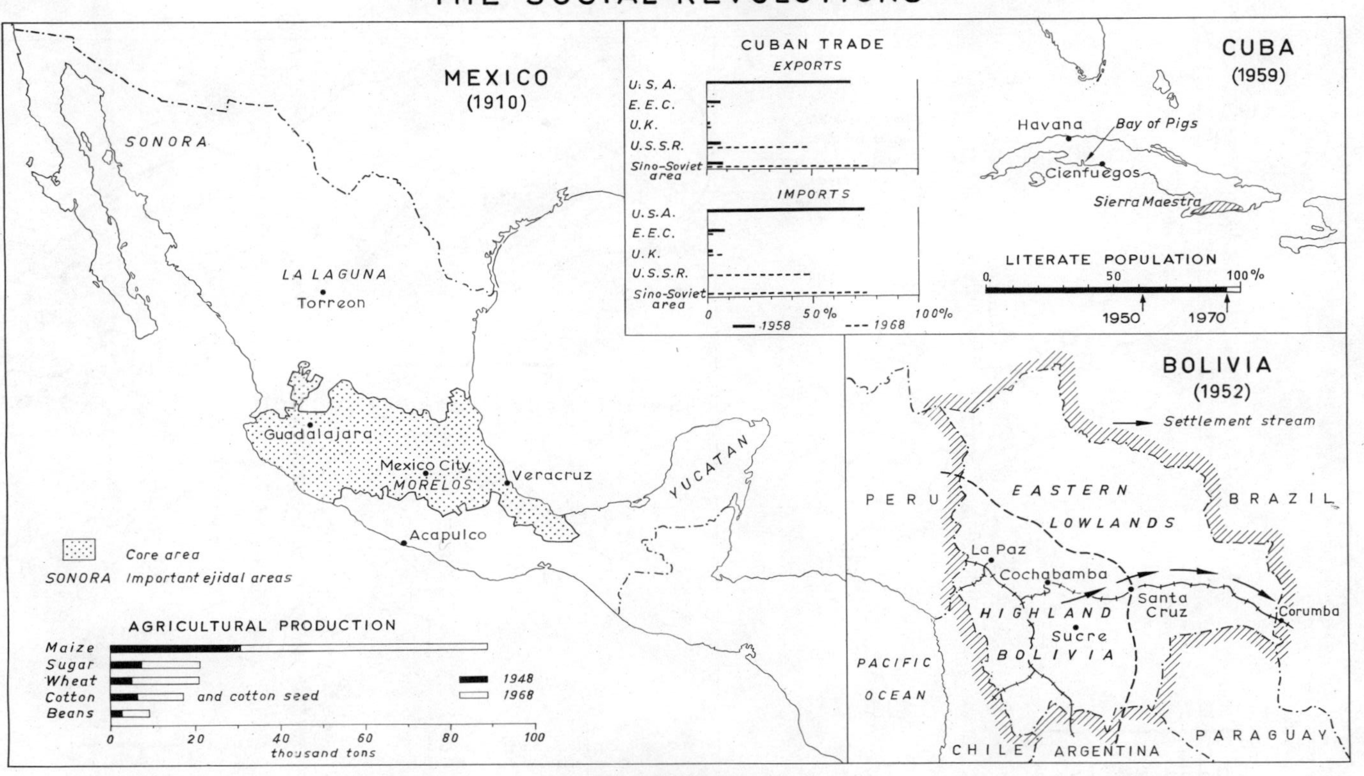

Fig. 12. *The Social Revolutions: Bolivia, Mexico, Cuba*

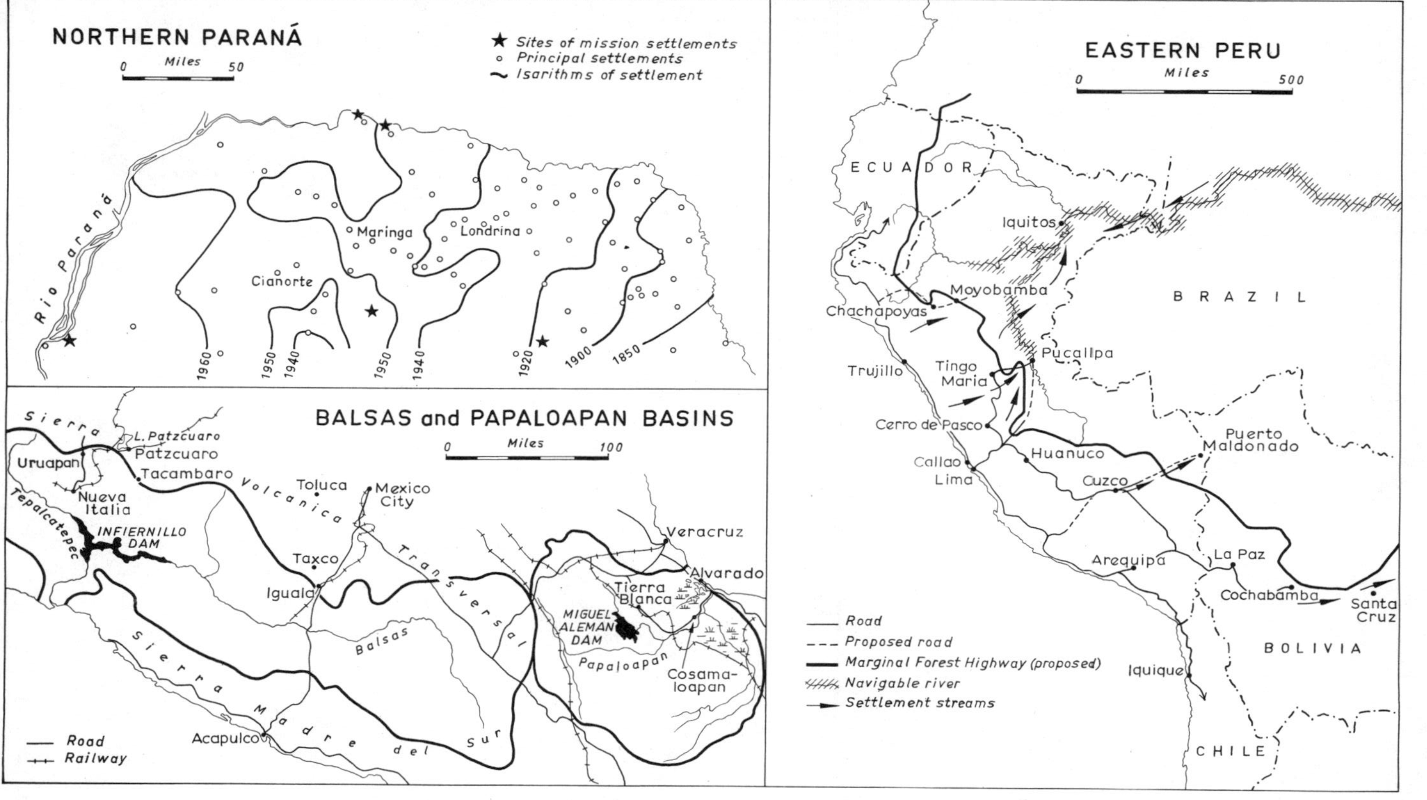

Fig. 13. *Internal Colonisation: the Andean fringe: Northern Paraná: Southern Mexico*

Even more spectacular changes in the demographic map have occurred in the last thirty years in south and central Brazil, in the states of Paraná and Goias. Here a great tide of settlement has swept across the rolling acres of Brazil's South-west, producing a well-balanced pattern of rural and urban living, of mixed farming, of commercial agriculture and increasing industrialisation. Planned and intelligent investment in agrarian settlement, urban development and roads by the *Companhia de Melhoramentos Norte do Paraná* and the pioneer efforts of Brazilians, many of them of Japanese origin, have converted the empty land of Paraná into Brazil's premier coffee state and fastest growing frontier land. Londrina, the capital of northern Paraná, founded in 1934, now has a population of 250,000 and a central business district of high rise buildings overlooking a land transformed beyond all belief. Maringá, the new western metropolis, did not exist at the end of the Second World War but is now a city of 120,000, serving a population of half a million in an area nearly as large as Tasmania. No less spectacular is the even more recent growth of the state of Goias, considerably helped by the creation of Brasilia and the westward shift of the nation's political centre of gravity. The state's population growth is the greatest in Brazil and its capital Goiania has tripled from 150,000 to 450,000 in the last ten years.

Important as these redistributions are, the magnitude of the problem of over-populated areas has not diminished, and some parts of the continent are conspicuously severe examples. Foremost in this respect are the three large islands of the Greater Antilles, Hispaniola, Jamaica and Puerto Rico. Relatively, Cuba is not over-populated, and with a more diversified agricultural economy, plus industrialisation, there should be few difficulties in providing a livelihood for its 8½ million population. The other islands, however, with a much more mountainous terrain are case studies of ever mounting population on inadequate land resources. Jamaica and Haiti with 2 and 5 million population respectively, each have about 450 persons per square mile of all land. If this is considered, however, from the point of view of population density per square mile of arable land, the density is nearer 2,500. It may be argued that this includes the urban populations of both states, but if these are ignored, the density of rural persons per square mile of arable land still reaches the very high figure of 1,500.

In Jamaica, the development of rich reserves of bauxite since the end of the Second World War has done much to bolster the economy. Jamaica also continues to be an important earner of foreign exchange from tourists and a relatively important source of agricultural exports, sugar alone accounting for one-fifth of all exports.

Haiti's total exports, are little more than one-eighth of those of Jamaica, in spite of its much larger population, and even these exports are largely dependent on the uncertain world market for coffee. In addition its tourist industry is now virtually non-existent. It is not surprising, therefore, that Haiti's per capita gross national product of less than eighty Australian dollars is less than half that of any other Latin American state and has remained virtually static, or even declined, in the last decade. It is a culture of rural poverty unequalled in the continent and directly the result of excessive population coupled with under-development.

The Dominican Republic, with 4 million people, or a density of some 700 rural persons per square mile of arable land, has a little more breathing space, but its economic position, totally dependent on agriculture and predominantly on sugar, is so inferior to that of Jamaica that its gross national product per capita is half that of the smaller island.

In the case of Jamaica and the other islands of the British Commonwealth, emigration to the United Kingdom in the 1950s and 1960s provided some relief to population pressure, but with the increasingly severe immigration restrictions introduced into Great Britain (and also into the United States) these escape valves have, to a great extent, been closed off.

The fact that these states are islands, with much inhospitable mountain terrain, and the maintenance of high population growth rates, exceeding 2.0 in Haiti, 2.5 in Jamaica and 3.5 in the Dominican Republic, appear to preclude any change for the better in the foreseeable future. The history of Puerto Rico, however, in the last twenty years does show what can be accomplished, given wise leadership, high investment, planned development programmes and population control. Much of the terrain of this, the smallest of the Greater Antilles, is not favourable for agriculture, and there are few mineral resources. With 2.7 million people, population densities of almost 800 per square mile, and of 1,400 rural persons per square mile, are very high. In the 1930s it had the reputation of being the slum of the Caribbean, largely because of the appalling housing conditions in the island and the depressed sugar monoculture which held its people in the grip of economic depression. Tens of thousands emigrated to New York, a relief made possible by the United States citizenship of the Puerto Ricans.

Since 1942, however, under the leadership of Muñoz Marín, "Operation Bootstrap" has literally pulled the island up by its own efforts and the investment of much United States capital. Agricultural diversification, industrialisation, the development of a tourist industry, birth control, and the rehousing of the population have transformed the picture beyond all recognition, and converted a predominantly agricultural island into a predominantly manufacturing state, for 60 per cent of goods produced are industrial products. The per capita gross national product has doubled in the last decade from 600 to 1,200 Australian dollars, easily the highest of all Latin American states. Real income trebled in the 1940-65 period. Population growth rates have been considerably reduced (despite one of the world's lowest crude death rates) to a figure comparable with that of Australia, taking into account Australia's flow of immigrants.[1] More than $1\frac{1}{4}$ million tourists visit the island annually, making it second only to Mexico in the income earned from this source. Its energy consumption is greater than that of the total of all the six Central American republics and electricity production exceeds that of Cuba or Peru. Cement output, the index of constructional activity, is greater only in Brazil, Mexico, Argentina, Colombia and Venezuela. Life expectancy around the seventy mark for males and females is the highest in the continent.

These indices do not mean that Puerto Rico has solved all its problems, for there is still much poverty, and a quarter of the houses still lack piped water inside or outside the dwelling; a fifth of the population is illiterate; and tuberculosis is still a menace to be fought. Average per capita income is still only half that of Australia or one-third that of the United States. Many former emigrants, attracted by the island's increased prosperity, have returned home and unemployment is still high.

Nor must it be forgotten that the "advantages" of Puerto Rico are enjoyed by no other part of Latin America—vast United States investment, often running at 250 million dollars annually during the 1960s, income from United States military bases and a preferential tariff market in the United States for its industrial and agricultural products.

Much of the high pressures of population on limited land resources are the result of long occupance, as for example, in the Caribbean examples just quoted, where settlement has persisted for more than four and a half centuries. There were also few opportunities for out-migration throughout this period into adjacent empty lands. Another example on the mainland proper is derived from a similar long, continuous period of colonial

[1]Australia's birth rate 19.4 per 1000: Puerto Rico's 26.2.

occupance, namely North-east Brazil which was the economic heart of the Portuguese Empire. Salvador, the capital, was founded as early as 1502, and Recife, sixty years later. These cities were the cornerstones of Brazilian economic prosperity, built upon sugar plantations, financed by Portuguese *haciendados* and worked by imported Negro slaves. Together these two cities contain over 2 million people, and in all Brazil only Rio de Janeiro, São Paulo, Belo Horizonte and Porto Alegre are larger. In addition Fortaleza with 960,000 people, Maceio with 237,000, Natal with 265,000, and João Pessoa with 203,000 are all major cities.

These large populations are in part a result of four and a half centuries of occupation of a generally favourable landscape not dissimilar to that of coastal Queensland; in part the result of exceptionally high birth rates, much above Brazil's national average, whereby in several states of the North-east, half the population is under twenty years of age; and in part the result of migration of folk from the areas of unreliable rainfall in the interior of the North-east. Again like Queensland drought and flood are alternate menaces to a steady and continuous economic prosperity of Brazil's *sertão*. Under increasing adversity stemming from the combination of unreliable climate and growing population, the interior has become increasingly an area of emigration, both to the coastal cities and to other parts of Brazil.

Drought and flood have always been the great physical hazards of the area and the dislocations to the economy caused by them have for centuries led to mass emigration. In the past the coastal cities were the nearest and most obvious destinations, sometimes on a temporary basis until conditions in the *sertão* improved, more often to swell permanently the over-large populations of those cities. As other economic attractions have offered, the periodic out-migration spread to other parts of Brazil. Over 50,000 went into Amazonia in the early years of the rubber boom; the industrial labour market of Rio de Janeiro and São Paulo has become the magnet of the last quarter century and attracted 200,000 in the drought year of 1952. This movement intensified during the worst drought of the century in 1970.

The penetration of a more effective road system into and through the North-east has released additional outward currents of people who were previously dissuaded by difficulties of transport from moving far afield. This applies both to the coastal lands and the interior plateau lands, and many emigrants by rail, lorry, river boat and/or on foot are swelling the urban concentrations of South-eastern Brazil and relieving the demographic pressures of the North-east.

Although efforts have been and are being made to industrialise the North-east, especially by the provision of electric power from the Paulo Afonso falls on the São Francisco, the amounts of capital needed to revitalise the whole economic fabric of the North-east are enormous. The rehabilitation of the region by the integrated development of mining, irrigated agriculture and industry and by the provision of social needs and housing of a vast population cannot be accomplished overnight. For a long time to come Brazil's North-east will continue to be a vivid example of Latin American over-population in relation to its currently developed natural resources.

To Australians the magnitude of the problem may be gauged by a comparison with Queensland with which there are many natural similarities. The area of Brazil's North-east (one-fifth of all Brazil but containing one-third of its population) is very similar to that of Queensland. Today (1972) the states of the North-east contain some 35 million people, Queensland less than 2 million. Moreover the population of Brazil's North-east continues to grow at approximately one million annually.

The political implications of too many people on too little land, deriving from lack of employment opportunities, congestion and a whole complex of socio-economic problems are self-evident. It is little wonder, therefore, that North-east Brazil and the West Indies have been principal foci of political discontent in Latin America.

4

Latin America has begun its industrial revolution without having undergone an agricultural revolution.

JACQUES CHONCHOL

People and Food

Agricultural stagnation: malnutrition: food imports: *latifundia* and *minifundia:* agrarian reform: Mexico, Bolivia and Cuba: the empty lands.

Despite the population problems outlined in the previous chapter, there is no reason why Latin America should not be able to provide enough food for its growing population and to have available considerable surpluses of raw materials and food for export. The natural resources are there and, given wise utilisation, are sufficient to feed the continent's total population and cater for its rapid growth. With modern transport methods, even mal-distribution of population is no excuse by itself for the continent's tragic inability to meet its food requirements.

Agricultural stagnation could be viewed quite justifiably as Latin America's basic and most acute problem. It is so fundamental that unless it is solved, most of the other problems fall into an insoluble classification. Indeed most of the region's other problem's intermesh with the deficiency of nutrition experienced by more than half of the continent's population.

Beginning with man's most elemental need, water, it is estimated by international expert bodies such as the Pan American Health Organisation that over 150 million persons are without a supply of safe drinking water, and 90 per cent of the rural population and nearly half of the urban population live in houses without easily available drinking water. Since polluted drinking water is the principal source of intestinal diseases, it is hardly surprising that these rank as the leading cause of death among Latin American infants, and the principal killer in many states such as Mexico, Colombia, Ecuador, Hispaniola and the republics of Central America. The debilitating effects of these chronic diseases on such a scale mean "crippling economic losses to the nations concerned and obviously pose an awesome obstacle to progress."[1]

Perhaps even more serious and more widespread is the same effect on Latin America's economy of undernourishment or malnutrition or both. The average daily intake of the low-income rural groups throughout Latin America is about 1,600 calories per head compared with the United Nations' minimum requirement of 2,500 calories. Some 7 per cent of the continent's children suffer from severe malnutrition and another 45 per cent from moderate malnutrition. The average diet is mainly of carbohydrates and starches and lacks the basic requirements of animal protein, vitamins and minerals. These deficiencies stunt the growth of children, and in Bolivia for example one-third of new-born children are notably shorter than normal. Clinical tests in Chile also indicate that the average height of the population is actually declining as a result of undernourishment. Chile's infant mortality rate, owing chiefly to malnutrition, at 108 per 1000 births is one of the highest in the world and is some six times that of Australia. Shortage of proteins also causes dietary dystrophy, and about three-quarters of Lima's population show some signs of this deficiency.

The table on p. 44, which has been constructed to show both the estimated food requirements per capita, and the actual levels consumed, indicates how near most of the population is to minimum needs, especially if one takes into account that they are *average* figures and, therefore, that some sections of the population consume considerably in excess of the minimum needed. The requirements vary because of such factors as the age and sex distribution of the population and the average annual environmental temperature.[2] More important in some ways than total quantity of food is the nutritional quality of the diet, and most significant in this respect is the protein quantity, as it is not only a source of energy but also is essential for maintenance of body tissues and for growth. Foods which are rich in proteins derived from animal sources are especially useful indicators of the nutritional quality of diets, and are therefore included in the following table.

From the table it will be seen that in all Latin America only Argentina and Uruguay can be considered as having adequate foodstuffs quantitatively and nutritionally.

[1]*Statistical Abstract of Latin America, 1967*. Latin American Center, U.C.L.A., 1969, p. 16.

[2]If the U.N. average 2,500 calories is taken as the "requirement", only Mexico, Argentina, Brazil, Paraguay, Uruguay and Cuba exceed it.

FOOD NEEDS AND CONSUMPTION

Country	*Estimated requirements in calories*	*Consumption*	*Consumption as per cent of requirements*	*Protein levels*	
				Total	*Animal*
Mexico	2450	2600	106.1	72.0	23.4
El Salvador	2310	2030	87.9	56.7	15.1
Guatemala	2330	2040	87.6	54.3	8.7
Honduras	2300	2080	90.4	53.6	12.7
Panama	2370	2310	97.5	58.1	23.5
Dominican Republic	2340	2040	87.2	49.7	19.2
Jamaica	2375	2250	94.7	57.9	22.5
Argentina	2580	2820	109.3	81.6	52.4
Bolivia	2420	1810	74.8	47.3	11.5
Brazil	2310	2780	120.3	66.3	18.0
Chile	2560	2410	94.1	77.2	27.3
Colombia	2440	2170	88.9	49.3	22.8
Ecuador	2330	1890	81.1	48.5	17.0
Paraguay	2280	2560	112.3	64.0	24.6
Peru	2480	2320	93.5	57.6	18.0
Uruguay	2580	2970	115.1	94.5	61.9
Surinam	2410	1980	82.2	44.5	15.1
The comparable figures for Canada, the United States and Australia are:					
U.S.A.	2590	3200	119.7	96.2	64.9
Canada	2640	3180	114.4	96.3	60.4
Australia	2570	3120	117.5	92.1	60.1

Part of these deficiencies is the result of a considerable reluctance to change dietary habits. Most rural Mexicans grow maize, often of poor quality, irrespective of the suitability of the terrain and soils, because maize flour is the traditional basis of their diet. The dependence of people of the humid tropics on starchy roots, especially manioc, is another case in point. The neglect of fisheries is a further reason why the consumption of animal proteins is so low, but inadequate marketing, transport and distribution facilities obviously restrict the opportunities for inland populations to consume this important source of food.

The principal cause, however, of the inadequate production of foodstuffs from a continent capable of a vastly greater output is the stagnation in the agricultural sector of the economies of most of the republics. A variety of conditions has produced this state of affairs. Increasing emphasis on industrialisation as the key to economic prosperity has led to a neglect of agriculture in many countries. This has been evident in the relative failure of technology to improve productivity, the low fertiliser consumption, and the increasing reliance of many nations on imports of foodstuffs. Chile is a conspicuous example of the latter. Once an exporter of grain, the nation was self-sufficient in respect of all foods which could be grown within the country until the mid-1950s. Today over one-quarter of the republic's imports are food, two-thirds of which could be grown within the country. This now benefits Australia which has begun to supply Chile with wheat, but the burden on Chile's limited foreign exchange can only continue to handicap its economic development. Even Argentina was compelled in 1969 to buy 200,000 tons of wheat from Australia to meet its shortage. Peru is in a similar situation. In 1968 23 per cent of the country's imports were food, compared with an average 17 per cent in the previous four years. The total food import bill in 1968 therefore denuded the foreign exchange by 130 million Australian dollars, with wheat and meat as the major items. A study made jointly by the Peruvian Ministry of Agriculture, the Agency for International Development and two United States universities has forecast that Peruvian food imports will triple in cost by 1980.[1]

The fundamental cause of this failure of agricultural production to keep pace with rapid population growth is the inherent under-utilisation of land, water and manpower, which is the direct result of the whole structure of agriculture in Latin America. Not only are there tens of thousands of farms that are too small, too isolated and too poor to be run as economic units—the problem of *minifundia*—but there are vast estates, relics of an extensive colonial pastoral tradition, held by their owners almost for prestige purposes and producing but a fraction of what the land is capable of yielding—the problem of *latifundia*. These twin problems and all their associated and derived social, economic and political problems have affected or still affect all the republics of Latin America. Mexico, Bolivia and Cuba have attempted a widespread radical attack on this agricultural malaise, in each case with undoubted social benefit therefrom, but with variable economic benefits. Encouraged or threatened by these examples, almost every other unit of Latin America has formulated a programme of agrarian reform, and aid from the Alliance for Progress has almost been dependent upon steps being taken in this direction. Few now dispute that the nature and distribution of rural property and income presents the greatest obstacle to the expansion of investment and technological change in agriculture.

The bulk of the rural population lacks any surplus income; nor does it possess sufficient land to permit an increase in

[1]*Bolsa Review*. Vol. 3, No. 34, Oct. 1969. p. 659

investment. Meanwhile the comparatively few who own most of the land and income seldom develop their property efficiently by increasing production or applying technological innovations. The profits made on the large estates are rarely re-invested. Usually this income is spent on urban investment, luxury consumption, and/or sent out of the country.[1]

The Inter-American Committee for Agricultural Development (CIDA) which is formed by the Food and Agriculture Organisation of the United Nations, the United Nations Economic Commission for Latin America, the Inter-American Development Bank, the Organisation of American States and its Institute of Agricultural Sciences has made analyses of land tenure and development and the nature of the agrarian problem in Argentina, Brazil, Chile, Colombia, Ecuador, Guatemala and Peru. These seven countries contain about two-thirds of Latin America's population and area. From this investigation it is clear that the number of family-operated farms characteristic of Western Europe and typical of much of Australia is very limited. They occur indeed in exceptional areas of specialised settlement like the south-central Chilean area of German occupation or the newly-settled areas of northern Paraná. Elsewhere most of the agricultural land is held in large estates and half the agricultural population is completely dependent upon these estates. "With no alternative employment or possibility of obtaining sufficient land of his own for subsistence the peasant is forced to work on the estate on the owner's terms."[2] The control of the estate-owners is autocratic. Not only do the local social, political, educational and even religious institutions depend upon their support and approval, but, because they control the lion's share of the agricultural land the estate owners receive the bulk of the agricultural credit, the benefit of government-financed irrigation schemes and rural extension services. The incidence of taxation falling upon them is very low, because for so long they have had enormous political influence. It is indeed amusing, in the midst of this widespread tragedy, how estate owners have assessed the value of their properties at very low figures to reduce even further the slight taxes they incur, and have then protested vigorously when reforming governments have accepted their valuations as the prices for compensation upon expropriation.

[1] *Statistical Abstract of Latin America, 1967,* Latin American Center, U.C.L.A., 1969, p. 32.

[2] Barraclough, Solon "The Agrarian Problem" in C. Véliz (ed.) *Latin America and the Caribbean: A Handbook,* London, 1968, p. 491.

Apart from the political and economic power possessed by the estate owners, the whole community structure is one of sharp social divisions which are little better than castes and, as has already been pointed out, the majority of the peasants have little opportunity for education and live in housing with no sanitation, safe water supply or rudimentary congenial comfort.

Although the fundamental economic weakness in the Latin American agricultural sector is the inability of the system to provide enough food for the undernourished millions of the continent, it will be seen that it is quite impossible to separate out the economic from the social and political ills of the system. Several decades ago Arnold Toynbee recognised that "in Latin America agrarian reform is the necessary starting point for political, economic and social change alike", and the three Latin American countries which have carried through a social revolution —Mexico, Bolivia and Cuba—have all identified agrarian reform as a central pivotal liberating force. The significance of the Mexican revolutionary slogan and the order of the words composing it, *Tierra y Libertad* still forms the motif of all those advocating radical change in agrarian structures in the other republics. The experiences of Mexico, Bolivia and Cuba, despite the mistakes, dislocations and crises suffered by them, cannot but give support to those who wish for a change from the centuries-old entrenched patterns which have become totally inadequate—socially, economically and politically—for the twentieth century.

It will be useful, therefore, if we summarise the achievements of these social revolutions in chronological order. Mexican agrarian reform in the last half century, especially under the six years of the rule of Cárdenas, 1934-40, liquidated the latifundia of that nation by distributing some 45 million acres in the form of *ejidos* (communal lands owned by groups of peasants) and in so doing eliminated the cause of persistent frustration and constantly incipient revolution. Moreover, despite a host of problems, lack of capital, irrigation works, mechanisation, management and organisation, the annual growth rate has been sufficient to achieve national self-sufficiency and to end the importation of food products such as maize, wheat and beans, and to leave a surplus for export. Agricultural, pastoral and fish production now contributes two-thirds of all Mexico's exports, especially prominent being the surpluses of coffee, cotton, sugar, fruit and vegetables, many of them produced under modern agricultural technology in ejido land tenure farms.

This does not mean that Mexico's rural problems have been solved. Rural over-population is still critical and industrial growth will have to absorb this surplus labour. With such demographic pressure there has been a renewed tendency to fragmentation of holdings, thus re-creating the problems of minifundia. There is still plenty of scope for the improvement of rural living conditions and for the growth of rural income. Yet, when one considers that in the post-revolutionary period the population of Mexico has grown from 15 to 50 millions, and that the social cohesion and political stability of this population can be added to the agricultural economic achievements just quoted, it would be remarkable if Latin Americans ignored the Mexican example.

Much of Mexico is high, mountainous and arid, so that it is an understatement to say that agriculture is difficult—but nearly all of populated Bolivia can be described in identical terms. If the balance sheet of agrarian reform there shows some credit entries, it should be an indication that it must succeed in more favoured lands. The period of post-revolutionary Bolivia is not yet twenty years in length, and in the 1950s agricultural production fell off, for social and political objectives were given priority over the economic needs of the country. There were also the inevitable deficiencies of technical advice, of agronomic experts and of co-ordinated programmes to reduce the population on the poor *altiplano* lands by resettlement in the rich tropical eastern half of the republic. As a result there were the usual trends towards fragmentation and further minifundia, and the illiterate Indian population did not at first take easily to modern cooperative or collective agriculture.

The pattern of agrarian reform involved six different types of land tenure, ranging from small family-operated farms through extensive pastoral ranches to communal undertakings. Already the recovery in agricultural production seems to indicate that soon Bolivia will not only be self-sufficient in foodstuffs but an exporter of tropical produce as the eastern areas are more fully settled. The leeway to be made up in the case of Bolivia is enormous, for the effects of centuries of neglect cannot be obliterated overnight.

The same applies to the social and political scene, and although there have been fluctuations in the relative power of the rural and urban workers, and frustration at the pace of progress, the political consciousness of the Bolivian peasantry provides a popular basis for government completely lacking until 1952. This found further expression on May Day, 1971, in the creation of the *asamblea del pueblo*. Of its 240 members, 60 per cent are elected by the labour unions and the remainder are drawn from student, peasant and middle-class professional organisations and the left-wing political parties.

It is virtually impossible for Bolivia, however, to overcome all its social deficiencies—especially in education and health—without international aid. Perhaps the most important single objective should be to provide a better economic structure, especially in respect of communications, to enable the nation to plan for sustained internal growth to provide a better society in the future.

Both the United Nations and the United States have done much in this direction. In fact the United Nations Technical Assistance programme in Bolivia has been one of the most important the United Nations has carried out anywhere in the world, for their international experts have not only worked in close collaboration with Bolivian governmental institutions but in an integrated form actually within those institutions. They have also secured the support of other international agencies in the programme such as the United Nations Educational, Social and Cultural Organisation, the International Labour Organisation, the Food and Agricultural Organisation and the World Health Organisation. The United Nations mission has included Americans, Canadians, Italians, Venezuelans and Australians; and Edmundo Flores, a Mexican, thoroughly familiar with Mexican agrarian reform, helped to establish the administrative organisation to implement similar reform in Bolivia. The Andean Highlands Mission, sponsored by the International Labour Organisation, has extended technical aid to the peasants receiving land under the redistribution programme, and has initiated many interesting experiments in rural progress.

> The aim has been "to devise a workable combination of individual and cooperative methods for the organisation of agriculture. A blacksmith's shop has been set up to make improvements in the Indians hand tools. Schoolhouses have been built, largely by the labor of the children and their parents, and are in use both day and night. A small medical centre has been established. . . . One plan is to recruit groups of young Indian men and women who will come there for training in the rudiments of agriculture, health and education and then return to their own communities to put their knowledge into practice."[1]

So Dr Carter Goodrich, the original negotiator of the United Nations Mission describes early efforts on an expropriated *hacienda* of 28,000 acres where four hundred Indian families eked out an existence in the heart of the over-populated Lake Titicaca region. Often attempts to get the indigenous folk to use new techniques to

[1]Goodrich, C. *The Economic Transformation of Bolivia.* Ithaca, 1955, p. 31.

get more production from their holdings meet with the stubborn traditionalism of the peasants. Dr Alexander describes one such example:

> The Indians at first refused the offers of the United Nations people of better seeds and fertilizer, saying that they had always used their own methods and achieved good output and they saw no reason to change. So the head of Pillapi asked the Indians to let him plant with his methods land which they considered too poor to use. They agreed to this. When the output on the "wasteland" turned out to be much better than their own production, the peasants were convinced and became eager to get the new seed and to use fertilizer.[1]

The efforts of the United States Point Four programme in Bolivia were directed towards diversifying the Bolivian economy and making it less dependent on its mono-metal base. These included road construction, the training of technicians, agricultural development and the supply of surplus food stocks to the undernourished population. They are further examples of outside contributions to make the country more viable.

The third social revolution, that of Cuba, is only a decade old, and reactions to it, for and against, are so charged with ideological attachments that it is not easy to assess its effects. Before the revolution the sugar monoculture maintained an economy of a two-class society, the rich who owned the land and the poor who worked it. The latter lived at a subsistence level, and from the nature of sugar cultivation there was endemic unemployment. No Latin American country was bound economically so close to the United States—the land, the sugar factories, the supply of manufactured goods and the tourists all belonged to or were derived from Cuba's powerful neighbour. As one close observer of the Cuba scene succinctly summarised it: "Cuba earned millions of dollars—and lost her self-respect."[2]

As in the cases of Mexico and Bolivia, agrarian reform was a fundamental objective of the revolution, for economic, social and political reasons. And as in the cases of Mexico and Bolivia numerous mistakes were made. The conversion of the old sugar estates into cooperatives and collectives was easy, but there was a shortage of managerial and administrative skills, of fertilisers, of mechanical aids to agriculture, of technicians and of transport.

[1]Alexander, Robert J. *The Bolivian National Revolution*. Rutgers, 1958, pp. 249-50.
[2]Ferguson, J. Halcro. "Cuba" in Véliz, C. (ed.) *Latin America and the Caribbean: A Handbook*, London, 1968, p. 257.

Some of the attempts at agricultural diversification were hasty and ill-advised, and too much effort and investment were devoted to a rapid drive for industrialisation. During this severe period of adjustment the economy was maintained by the help of the Soviet Union, and the whole pattern of Cuban trade had to be completely reorientated from its American dependence to an East European dependence—a much more formidable problem than either Mexico or Bolivia had had to contend with.

The economic results to date are fairly clear. After a considerable dislocation and decline of the sugar industry, output is now approximately the same as before the revolution. There has been considerable diversification and the cattle and poultry industries have been reorganised and developed. A huge fertiliser plant is being constructed by a British firm. There has been a switch of much rural labour into industrial employment, but peasant productivity is still low. As regards food supplies, the total quantity of food available is probably less than before the revolution, due largely to the curtailment of imported food supplies on which Cuba was always dependent. Breakdowns in transport and inefficiency in the rationing system have also made the reductions in total food availability more evident. On the other hand all objective observers agree that food distribution is more equitable than before the revolution, and unlike Bolivia, Cuba's standard of living is well above the Latin American average.

It is, however, in the social fields that Cuba, like Mexico especially, has undoubtedly made enormous progress. There has been a phenomenal expansion of educational services, and without exception, Cuba has now become the most literate republic of Latin America.[1] Building priorities were switched from hotels and casinos to roads, schools, clinics and low-cost housing, and the most remote mountain settlement now is conscious that they are cared for, and that the Government unlike all previous governments, is no longer Havana-orientated. The number of hospital beds has more than doubled, and medical interns are obliged to practisc in rural areas.

Politically too much emotion enters into most assessments of the results of the revolution. That the regime has been driven into the Communist fold by a complete trade embargo and by attempted United States-sponsored invasion, few would deny. The reaction of the United States, largely for financial reasons, was totally different to the support that country gave to the similar revolution

[1]Only Mexico and Cuba of all Latin American republics have succeeded in reducing the absolute number of illiterates in their populations.

in Bolivia. The fact that Cuba is Communist should have been no greater reason for United States ostracism than for a similar attitude to Romania, which President Nixon visited so enthusiastically after his inauguration, or to Yugoslavia the recipient of considerable United States technical and financial aid.

Many thousands of Cubans, unwilling to remain under a Communist dictatorship, have left the country; and unlike Mexico and Bolivia there has been no attempt to restore democratic institutions. On the other hand there are fewer political prisoners than under the regime the revolution displaced, and there is a great national support for a persecuted regime. Two observers of the scene probably summarise the first decade of the revolution:

> On the credit side of the ledger are the facts that the average Cuban today is better fed, better housed and better educated than he ever was before. On the debit side are the mistakes and misguided experiments that led to an overambitious industrialisation plan which had to be scrapped at the cost of millions of dollars of scarce foreign exchange used to buy plant and equipment that now lie idle.[1]
>
> Economically, as politically, Cuba's situation is neither so rosy as her supporters claim nor so disastrous as her detractors insist.[2]

On balance, the reforms instituted by the three social revolutions in widely different countries provide social and economic advantages, and in the case of Mexico political advantages too, over the continued preservation of the status quo. Indeed no other solution has yet done so much to help feed, educate and care for the hungry millions of the continent. This simple message has reached all parts of Latin America. There is scarcely a government which has not introduced legislation providing for agrarian reform, often in republics where twenty years ago such an idea would have been anathema. Prodded by the Alliance for Progress, alarmed by the threat of a Cuban-type revolution, and increasingly made aware of the failure of the present agrarian structure to provide the goods for their increasing populations, the problem has been tackled with variable degrees of energy and determination over the continued resistance of the landowners. Progress to date, compared with the vast transformations carried out in Mexico, Bolivia and Cuba, can only be described as moderate, with the landed interests and their political representatives urging delay

[1]Economist Intelligence Unit. Jan. 1967.
[2]Ferguson, J. op. cit., p. 252.

and the radical reformers deploring the slow progress being made. However, even the repressive Brazilian regime has found it necessary to effect some agrarian reform, Peru's military leaders have pressed ahead with land distribution, and the steps initiated by Frei to break the stranglehold of Chile's haciendas have been accelerated by Allende's socialist regime.

The combination of the social and economic disadvantages of this long-perpetuated latifundia system, the overthrow of the system in Mexico, Bolivia and Cuba, and the relative slowness and inefficacy of the agrarian reform measures so far instituted in the other republics, has produced an atmosphere of crisis in many parts of the continent. Here and there the crisis has erupted in direct action by the peasants. The invasion of haciendas in the Peruvian Sierra has been a continuing movement during the 1960s; the same process has been going on in Ecuador in a less publicised form; the political unrest in Colombia, Guatemala and El Salvador has an important agrarian protest component; and in Brazil's North-east the formation of the Peasant Leagues was a mass movement in support of better rural wages and working conditions. There is no doubt that the political subservience of the rural masses of Chile to their patron's wishes is rapidly disintegrating, and that the support of that republic's rural population for the Socialists and Communists is increasing. Indeed this support was fundamental in securing the election of President Salvador Allende in October, 1970.

Perhaps too much emphasis is placed on the redistribution of land. The problem is a much wider one—the under-utilisation of land and labour, the lack of investment in agriculture, the low contribution made by the estates to government revenue, the non-participation of the workers in the money economy of the country, the inefficiency of social welfare legislation to improve the peasant's lot, and the increasing rural population despite the steady migration to the cities. No problem is so widespread in its impact on the whole of Latin America, and no solution to it can be possible without national cooperation of all sectors of the population. The likelihood of this, in the climate of every group defending its own interests, seems more like myth than reality; and the future political possibilities developing from this situation will be discussed in a later chapter.[1]

[1]Leonard Gross in his study of Eduardo Frei, *The Last, Best Hope* on pp. 149-50 tells how the Conservative and Liberal senators tried to bargain their support of Frei's copper bill "if he would modify the method of determining property values for purposes of compensation under the proposed agrarian reform law."

5

Latin America contains within itself many of the problems that currently divide the rich and the poor nations of the world.

DAVID HUELIN

Economic Problems

Terms of trade: single commodity dependence: economic nationalism and industrialisation: foreign investment: inflation: the Latin American Free Trade Association and the Central American Common Market.

The more or less stagnant state of Latin American agriculture is undoubtedly one of the major impediments to the balanced economic growth of the region; but it is obvious that the facts of some of the associated consequences of the rural malaise, such as low purchasing power, limited reinvestment in agriculture and the migration to the cities cannot be limited to the rural sectors of the republics concerned. The situation would be bad if these agrarian-derived ills were the only economic problems facing Latin America, but unfortunately backwardness in the agricultural sector is just one aspect of a whole complex of economic tentacles which are crippling the progress of the continent. It is indeed difficult to know where to begin to untangle the intermeshed brakes on economic growth, but undoubtedly the dependence of all the republics on the export of primary products is fundamental. In a dozen of the countries a single commodity accounts for more than half of their total exports—Cuba, sugar; Bolivia, tin; Chile, copper; Colombia and Haiti, coffee; the Dominican Republic, sugar; Ecuador, Honduras and Panama, bananas; Trinidad and Venezuela, petroleum; and Uruguay, wool. Only Mexico can claim real diversity of exports. All the other republics have half or more of their exports made up of two commodities only (Fig. 14). This is, of course, a perilous situation for any nation to

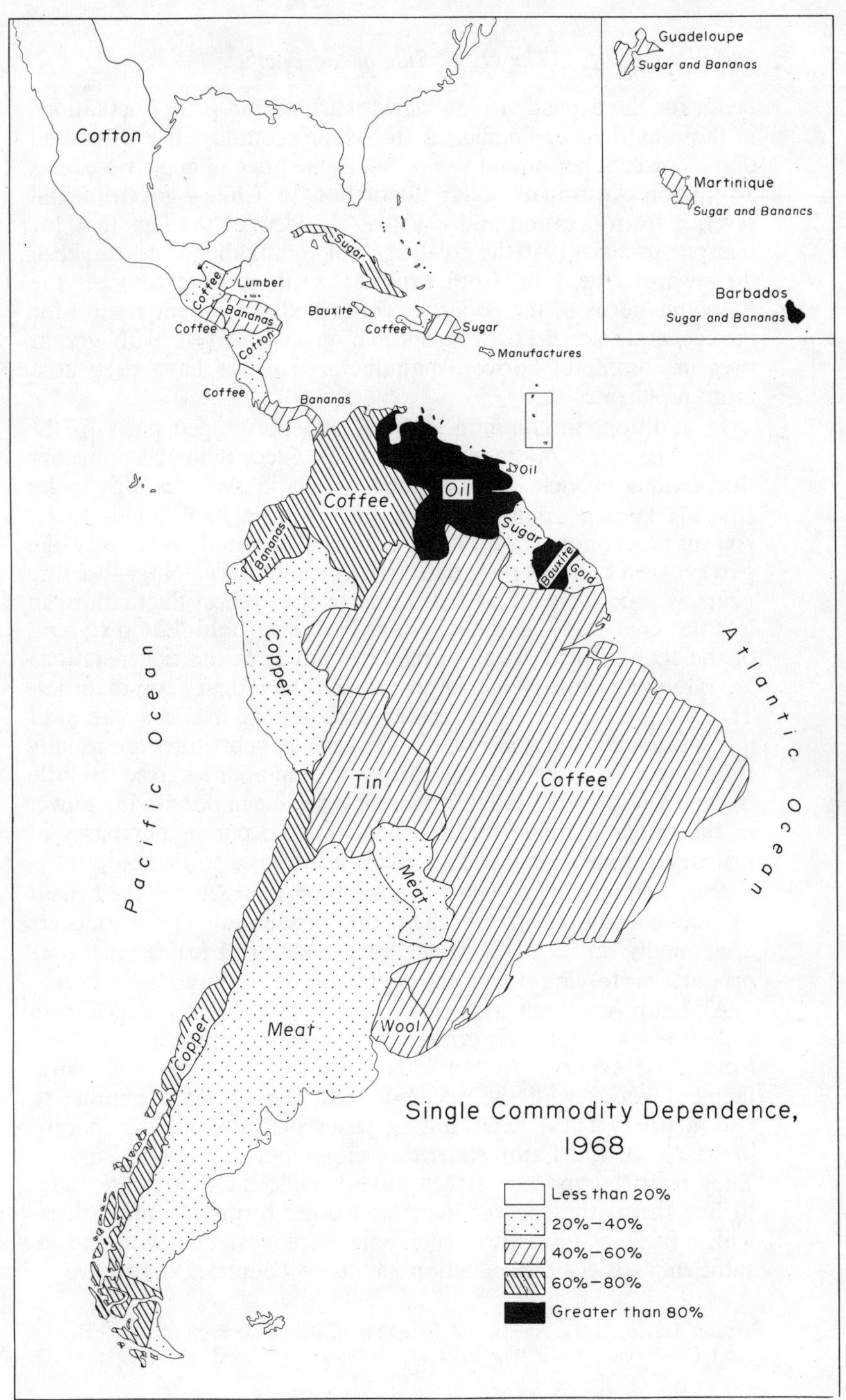

Fig. 14. *Single Commodity Dependence*

be in, for the dependence on world markets and price fluctuations in those markets can endanger the whole economy. It is estimated that a one cent per pound rise or fall in the price of copper means a 14 million Australian dollar fluctuation in Chile's governmental revenue from taxation and royalties. In view of the fact that for many years since 1950 the great trend of commodity prices has been downwards, the yield from exports has done little to meet the economic needs of the countries concerned, and is one reason for the general slowness of economic growth. Even with recent rises in commodity prices, manufactured prices have risen at a more rapid rate.

In addition, in common with all underdeveloped parts of the world, the terms of trade have a wider effect than the monetary fluctuations in yield from exports. In Latin America this wider effect is known as the Prebisch Effect, after Raúl Prebisch, an Argentine economist. In short it is one explanation of why the gap between rich and poor nations is constantly widening—because primary producers are at the mercy of the cyclical fluctuations in international trade, and always are forced to hold "the dirty end of the stick". Increases in purchasing power in the richer nations are rarely the cause of increased demand for primary commodities. The demand is rather for manufactured consumer goods, and even if this threatens a rise in raw material prices, substitutes are usually found, so exporters of the primary commodities receive little benefit. On the other hand, if there is a decline in purchasing power in the richer nations, the first economies occur in purchases of primary commodities, as the easiest economies to be made.

Even commodity agreements are arranged largely for the benefit of the consumers rather than the producers. The producers are usually in a weak bargaining position because of over-production forcing them to negotiate on a buyer's market.[1]

All Latin American countries, therefore, suffer not so much from lack of markets for their primary commodities, but lack of income from these exports. At the same time they have to buy manufactured goods with the proceeds, and these goods continue to rise in price. These deteriorating terms of trade are the shadow in which all the Latin American economies attempt to survive. They restrict imports, as they have insufficient foreign exchange to buy them; they accept loans and other forms of indebtedness which further strain their economic resources; and with the insufficiency of food production in many countries they have to

[1]Huelin, David, "Latin America: A Summary of Economic Problems" in Véliz, C. (ed.) *Latin America and the Caribbean: A Handbook*. London, 1968, pp. 472-3.

The racial components of Latin America's population are extraordinarily diverse. Haiti's 5 million negroes are descendants of slaves imported from Africa.

The Plaza of the Three Cultures, Mexico City, indicative of the three periods of occupance of the country: the indigenous foundations, the colonial church and the modern apartment building.

Pressure of population on land resources is most severe in the West Indies. High rural population densities compel villagers to use the slopes of mountainous lands—the Yallahs Valley of Jamaica.

Bananas on the quay at Guayaquil. Ecuador is the world's greatest exporter of this fruit, the product of small farms, unlike the plantation system in operation in most Caribbean countries.

Subsistence agriculture and the internal disposal of the products constitute the principal economic activities of Latin America's rural population. A roadside market in Haiti.

District agronomists discuss the agricultural programme with the foreman of an ejido near Torreón in central north Mexico. Agrarian reform is a cornerstone of the country's social revolution.

Since the end of the Second World War, the more developed countries of Latin America have acquired an industrial base. Volta Redonda between Rio de Janeiro and São Paulo is the continent's greatest iron and steel plant.

A new housing development in Santiago, Chile. An estimated 80 million people in the continent lack the most elementary type of adequate housing. (Photo Lan Chile)

In spite of migration to the cities, Latin America's rural population continues to grow in absolute numbers. Housing is usually primitive and congested—Montego Bay, Jamaica.

The world's largest concrete roof supported on a single pillar. The entrance to Mexico's Anthropological Museum containing a vast collection illustrating pre-conquest Mexican culture—an example of the renaissance accompanying the country's social revolution.

Mural on the School of Medicine, University City Mexico offers outstanding examples of mural sculptures and painting, depicting Mexican history and society.

A street in old San Juan. Puerto Rico was for almost four centuries under Spanish control. Now, as an "associated state" with the United States, a new San Juan, catering especially to its tourist trade, co-exists with and is adjacent to the old city.

São Paulo, Latin America's greatest city of over 6 million people, epitomises the modern, spacious commercial and industrial metropolises which attract folk from the overcrowded countryside.

Cuba's Fidel Castro waves to a cheering crowd as he leaves Santiago's airport with Chile's President Salvador Allende. (Photo Associated Press Ltd.)

Lázaro Cárdenas, Mexico's dynamic president 1934-40. His political, social and agrarian reforms gave a massive impetus to Mexico's social revolution. (Photo Associated Press Ltd.)

spend more of their limited foreign exchange on food imports instead of capital equipment to raise their own productive capacity.

There continues, too, to be a long-established reluctance of Latin American investors to risk capital in their own countries, except at fantastic rates of interest, or in real estate which increases in value proportionately to inflationary trends. The motives for the practice of "exile insurance" in the form of bank accounts in Europe are political, speculative and protective, but whatever the motives, it exacerbates a situation where domestic capital is insufficient.

Foreign capital to stimulate economic growth is decreasingly welcome in Latin America. There are wide variations between countries both in respect of governmental attitudes and the type of economic development involved. One of the few countries which in the last twenty years has encouraged considerable foreign investment has been Peru, but one of the principal reasons for the overthrow of the Belaúnde government in 1968 was the concern of many that the nation was becoming too tied to foreign interests.

Oil has been a particularly sensitive field for foreign involvement, as there is real concern about the control by international oil companies of domestic oil production. In every political change In Argentina since Perón, the subject of foreign investment in oil has been involved. The nationalistic slogan of *"O petroleo es nosotros"* (the oil is ours) in Brazil has resulted in rigid exclusion of foreign capital in that field, despite Brazil's great outlay on imported petroleum. In Mexico and in Chile, control of oil production has been secured for the nation by the replacement of, or avoidance of, foreign concessions respectively. The "Chileanisation" of Chile's copper production on a 51/49 basis by Frei's Christian Democratic government, followed in 1971 by outright nationalisation by Allende's socialist administration, is another indication of how Latin American nations are unwilling to have their economic resources developed by foreign capital when it means that investment equals control. The more recent questioning, by a variety of politicians in Australia, of the extent to which our oil, gas, iron ore and other mineral resources are passing into foreign control, is a similar manifestation of the concern about how far a nation should be dependent on overseas interests in the long run.

An interesting sidelight on this vital matter was given by Mr Charles Court, Western Australia's Minister for Industrial Development and the North-west, who in a recent visit to Brazil urged united action by the southern continents to prevent their conversion into "the world's quarry". His plea was that both Australia and Latin America should develop their raw materials in a processed or partly-processed form so providing increased income and employment.[1]

While it is true that there is considerable foreign investment, especially by the United States, and particularly in mining and oil development (Fig. 18), the total foreign investment in Latin America does not represent an enormous share of total investment. About one-third of the continent's economic activity is under governmental control and the remainder is privately owned. Of the latter, 90 per cent is owned by domestic capital and 10 per cent by foreign interests, most of these being in mining and manufacturing, and most in the three countries with the largest internal markets, Brazil, Mexico and Argentina.

A further inhibition on economic growth is the endemic nature of inflation in some of the Latin American republics. This is caused by many of the circumstances already discussed, and perhaps first and foremost is the shortage of essential foodstuffs and the shortage of manufactured goods demanded by the growing urban populations. Accompanying this increased demand is a lack of growth in savings, in investment, and in governmental revenue to match increased expenditures. These lead to a rising cost of living, demands for more wages and higher interest rates to cover loss of value of the currency, devaluations, speculation and unwillingness of potential investors to risk their capital. Mexico is one of the few countries not to devalue its currency; with others it has been almost an annual occurrence (Fig. 17).

It is small wonder that in this economic climate of primary commodity dependence, adverse terms of trade, lack of investment, stagnant agriculture and inflation, total economic growth has been little more than population growth. There are obviously variations from country to country, but in recent years the total increase in the gross national product has not been much above 4 per cent annually. With population increase at about 3 per cent, the real per capita income in most countries has only very marginally increased. Some of the Central American republics—due largely to the benefits of economic integration—and Mexico—due largely to the basic reforms and efficient administration resulting from its social revolution—are the countries experiencing the greatest economic growth (Fig. 15).

The sluggish pace of development as a whole comes from a combination of poor performances in all sectors of the economy.

[1] *The Guardian*. 19 November 1969.

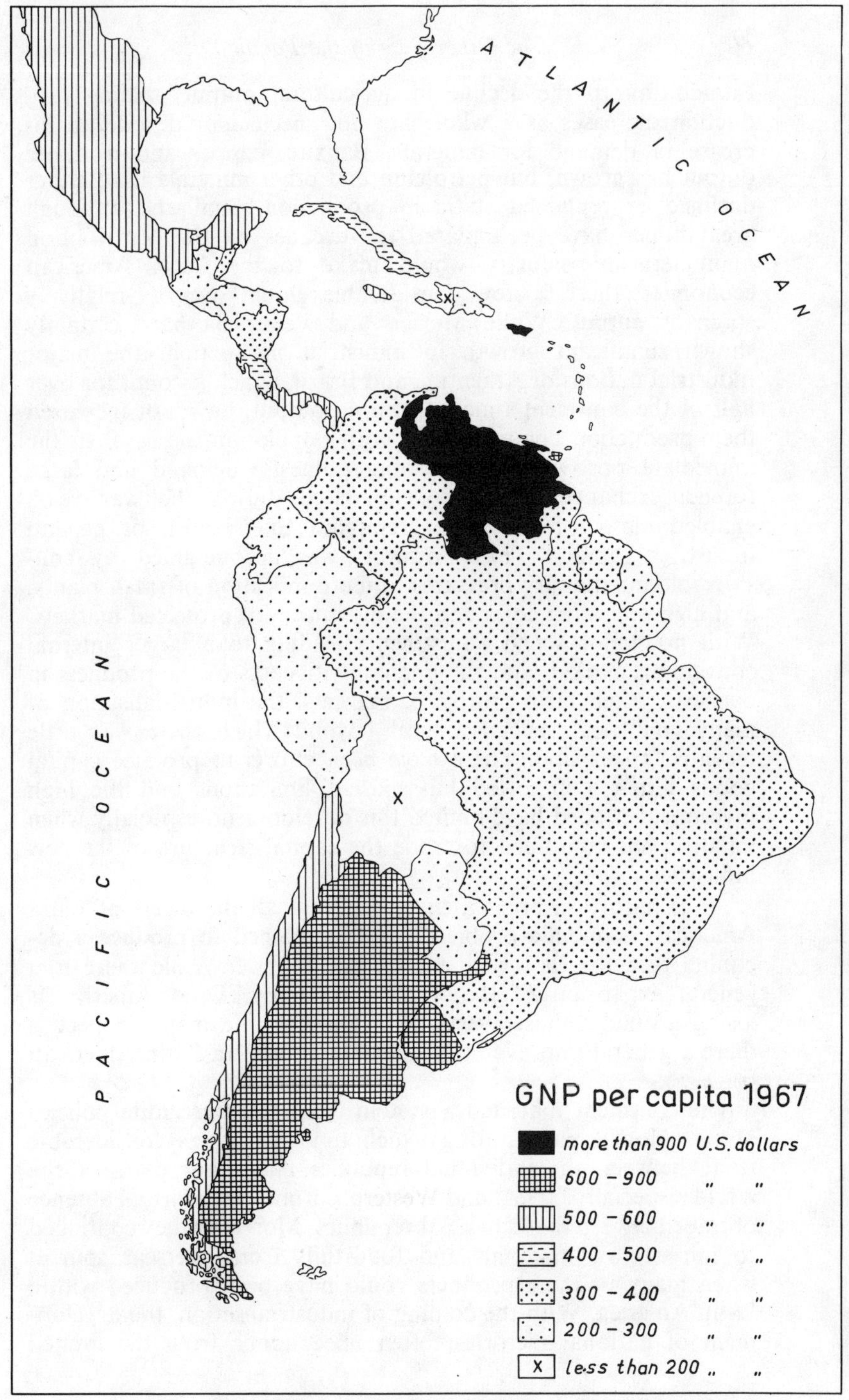

Fig. 15. *GNP of Latin America*

In addition to the decline in agricultural output, mining production increases as a whole are not spectacular despite an increase in demand for minerals. Bauxite, copper and iron ore output has grown, but petroleum and other minerals have either declined or remained static in production. Similarly, although great hopes have been placed for decades on the contribution manufacturing industry would make to the Latin American economies, there is now considerable gloom over its relatively stagnant output. While Mexico and Venezuela have certainly shown significant growth in industrial production, the major industrial nations of Argentina and Brazil, which account for over half of the continent's manufacturing output, have not increased their production commensurate with population increase. In the immediate post-war years, strong domestic demand and large foreign exchange reserves accumulated during the war years enabled many of the larger republics to establish or expand industries rapidly. This, however, was accompanied by considerable inflationary pressures, often duplication of small plants, and high operating costs and the institution of protected markets. With no major social adjustments leading to a larger internal consuming market, and the uncompetitiveness of the products in overseas, often tariff-protected, markets, the industrialisation of many countries reached a limit beyond which there was little incentive to expand. There have been efforts to produce capital goods hitherto imported but market limitations and the high investment needed have limited this development, especially when inflation has continued to erode the capital structure of the new industries.

It is hardly surprising, therefore, that all the facets of Latin America's economic problems have combined to produce a declining role for the continent in world trade. While there is a general expansion of the world's economy, Latin America is losing ground almost everywhere. Only in one major respect is there a general improvement, and that is in intra-Latin American trade.

The continent inherited a system from the mercantile policies of its colonial past, during which time there was considerable trade between the individual republics and other parts of the world (especially U.S.A. and Western Europe) but a virtual absence of trade between the individual republics. Moreover they continued to import raw materials and foodstuffs from overseas sources when many of these products could have been produced within Latin America. With the coming of industrialisation, the development of national factories, often uneconomic from the limited

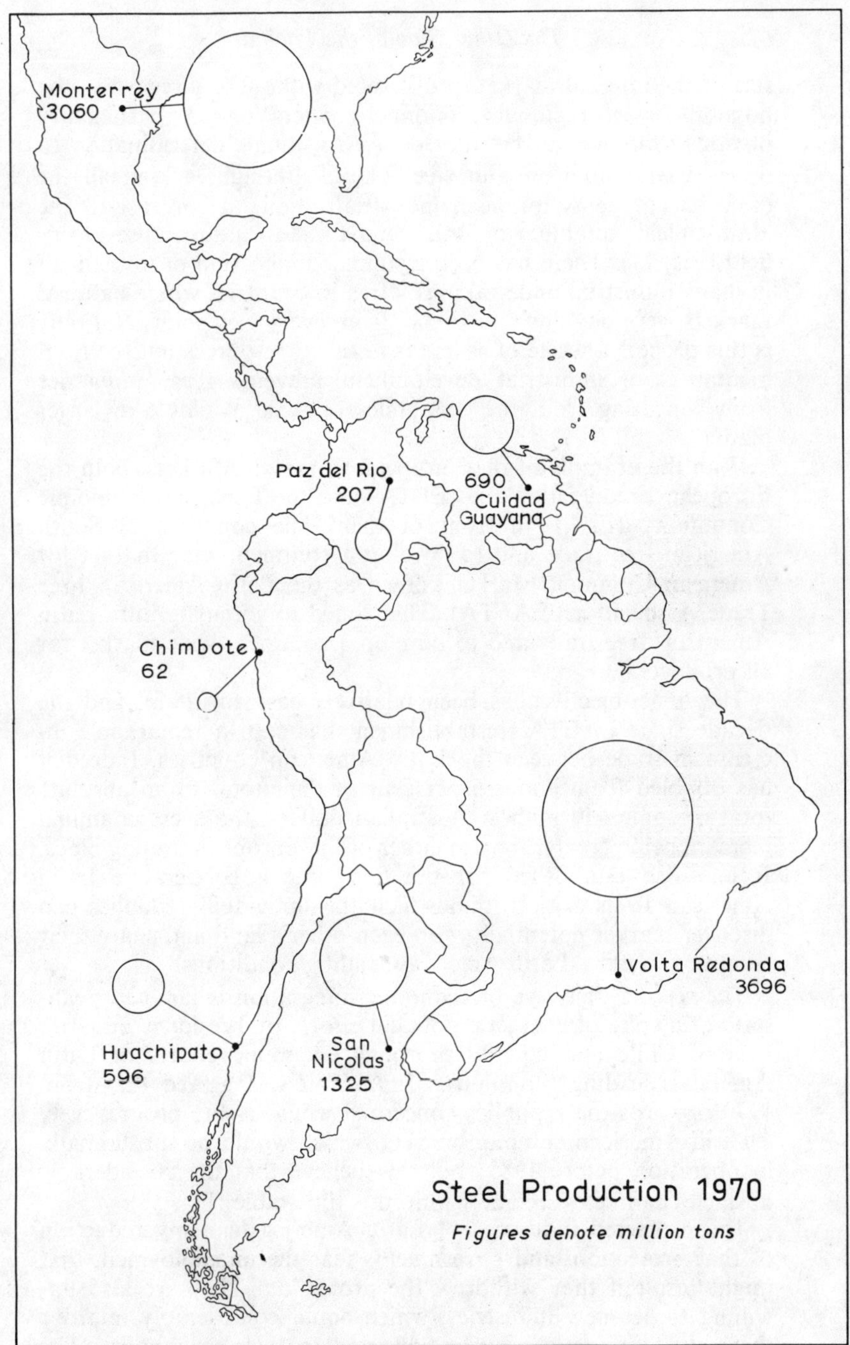

Fig. 16. *Steel Production*

size of the internal market, proliferated without any regard to the possibilities of regional economic cooperation. A particularly obvious example can be quoted of Argentina's determination to proceed with an iron and steel plant, although lacking all the basic requirements for such industrialisation, in contrast to the almost ideal suitability of Brazil and Chile to industrialise in this field (Fig. 17). There has been a similar duplication of investment in many industrial undertakings, often in countries where national markets were obviously too small from every viewpoint. Not only is this process a waste of scarce investment resources but the fragmentation of industrial development prevents these industries from benefiting from the economies of scale available in larger plants.

With the example of the European Common Markets, both the European Free Trade Area (EFTA) and the European Economic Community (EEC), in front of them, the countries of South American free trade and to develop a continent-wide market for American Common Market known as the Latin American Free Trade Association (LAFTA). This aimed to stimulate intra-Latin American free trade and to develop a continent-wide market for all products.

The first objective has been relatively easy to attain, and the decade since LAFTA's establishment has seen a remarkable increase in trade between the Latin American countries. Indeed it has doubled from about 6 per cent of their total to an absolute total of some 650 million Australian dollars, the average annual increase being greater than in either of the European trading blocs. It has also established for the first time a cooperative Latin American framework within which the individual republics can discover market potentialities in each other's land and share their reactions to extra-Latin American trading conditions.

The second objective of economic integration is far from realisation, in spite of energetic political efforts by President Eduardo Frei of Chile and equally thorough economic efforts of Latin America's leading economists. In 1967 it was agreed that from 1970 onwards the republics concerned would create progressively a Latin American common market, which would be substantially in operation before 1985; but few believe that the considerable obstacles can be overcome within this time-table (Fig. 18).

The protected industries of Latin America fear any reduction of that protection, and governments fear the unemployment that might result if they withdrew the protection. They are also unwilling to see new industries, which could considerably improve their own economic position, diverted to their neighbours. The

Fig. 17. *Inflation*

less developed countries fear that integration will mean ever greater polarisation of industry in the present nuclei of industry—Buenos Aires, Santiago, Rio de Janeiro, São Paulo, Mexico City—and the more advanced nations becoming richer and the less developed poorer. The more advanced nations, too, are reluctant to agree to new industries or developments going to their less advanced neighbours, as they are aware of the large fund of unemployed labour and undeveloped areas and resources in their own lands. These difficulties may be derogatorily summed up as "nationalism", but with nations living so much on the margins of social, economic and political unrest they are real obstacles. If this be doubted, one has only to consider the reactions in prosperous Australia if in an ANZ common market an important industrial development were diverted say from New South Wales to North Island, New Zealand.

Even if these difficulties were overcome, the communications pattern between the Latin American republics in respect of roads, railways and rivers is limited and tenuous. The population distribution in the Andes, along the Atlantic coast and surrounding the capital nuclei means that there are limited international links. The international frontiers are for the most part in unpopulated areas—unlike Europe where most of the intra-European trade is carried by road, river or railway across or through densely populated frontier zones. Even the intra-Latin American maritime links suffer from poor port facilities, and, until there is a vastly increased trade, the disadvantages of limited cargoes. It is often more expensive to ship goods from one Latin American country to another than from Latin America to Europe or North America.

If to these difficulties one adds problems of variable inflation, different monetary policies, differing attitudes to foreign capital, then the obstacles to economic integration can be seen to be really formidable. On the other hand, the advantages to be gained are enormous. The massive economies that could be made in capital investment, the price reductions that would be possible, the benefits that would be reaped from a good regional infrastructure, particularly of transport, marketing facilities, and the scope for filling empty regions, are so great that many of Latin America's social, economic and political problems would be eased if their governments determined to work resolutely in this direction.

Many believe an intermediate stage would be the best immediate goal, namely integration between the Andean group of nations—Colombia, Venezuela, Ecuador, Chile, Peru and Bolivia—so that when this was achieved there would be a bloc comparable in economic strength with each of the big three—Brazil, Argentina

Fig. 18. *Economic Cooperation and U.S. Investment*

and Mexico. Then, at a subsequent stage, bargaining between four relatively well developed economic units would be more possible on a give and take basis. This has attractive possibilities, but it is doubtful if it is a feasible proposition without massive international financing and radical economic and social changes within the six Andean countries with all their difficult terrain, vast undeveloped resources, and near absence of intra-regional infrastructure.

Considerable progress, however, has been made with another regional group, that of the Central American republics (Fig. 18). In fact, they were the pioneers in Latin America in intra-regional cooperation as the Central American Common Market really began as far back as 1957. In that year the United Nations Economic Commission for Latin America (ECLA) was asked for assistance to institute a programme "to develop agricultural and industrial production and the transportion systems of their economies and the creation of larger markets through the exchange of their products, the coordination of their development plans and the establishment of enterprises in which all the countries, or some of them, might be interested".[1] At first a series of bilateral agreements heralded the inception of the Market, but in 1958 a treaty was signed to create at first a common market and then a customs union. Since then intra-Central American trade has grown from almost nothing to between one-fifth and one-quarter of the total imports of each of the five republics. Not only has there been an expansion of trade but many light manufactured goods are now produced within the group whereas formerly they were imported, and these now represent about 70 per cent of intra-regional trade. A beginning has also been made in establishing common policies of uniform prices for basic foodstuffs (maize, rice and beans) traded between the group's members, hydro-electric and telecommunications networks, a bank for economic integration and a monetary union. Altogether, in spite of its limitations, the cooperation has been successful in speeding development in one of the most backward regions of Latin America. There is a great deal yet to be done, and possibly in the future the bloc may be able to bargain effectively with the other parts of the LAFTA organisation. In the meantime it shows that regional integration would eliminate much wasteful economic fragmentation and provide the opportunities for tackling some of Latin America's problems resulting from its political fragmentation.

[1]Terms of request by Central American Republics to ECLA

CENTRAL AMERICA

	Area sq. miles	*Population Est. 1970*	*Population density per sq. mile*	*Population growth rate*	*Rural population per cent*	*Urban population per cent*	*Population and capital*
Guatemala	42,044	5.1	121	3.1	66	34	577
El Salvador	8,083	3.5	432	3.8	61	39	281
Honduras	42,277	2.7	63	3.5	77	23	171
Nicaragua	53,670	2.0	37	4.0	59	41	262
Costa Rica	19,653	1.9	100	3.7	65	35	339

	GNP $A per capita 1966	*Principal exports per cent 1967*				*Foreign trade 1967 ($A)*	
						Imports	*Exports*
Guatemala	273	Coffee	34	Cotton	16	188,000 (1966)	181,000
El Salvador	251	Coffee	48	Cotton	8	203,000	188,000
Honduras	206	Bananas	50	Coffee	14	153,000	137,000
Nicaragua	327	Cotton	38	Coffee	14	185,000	138,000
Costa Rica	387	Bananas	22	Coffee	38	174,000	130,000

	Trade with CACM 1966 (million $A)		*Development of import trade with CACM (million $A)*		
	Imports	*Exports*			
Guatemala	31	46	1951	9	—
El Salvador	47	53	1956	12	8
Honduras	29	18	1961	33	33
Nicaragua	29	14	1966	160	75
Costa Rica	21	23			

There were, of course, certain inbuilt advantages towards the Central American integration. Under colonial rule the present republics were parts of one larger administrative unit, the Captaincy General of Guatemala; at independence they became a federal republic which lasted for almost twenty years; and several attempts have been made in the last century to secure a restoration of their political or economic unity. Perhaps their demographic fragmentation into half a dozen population nuclei and lack of communications between them were the principal obstacles on which these attempts foundered. There are also population pressures, especially in El Salvador, as witness the conflict between that state and Honduras in 1969, which often strain amicable relations between them.[1]

But the factors which unite them are really more than those which divide them. They are all part of one major geographical region with similar constituents of terrain, people, culture and economic life. They all depend on agricultural export commodities, mainly coffee and bananas and to a lesser extent, cocoa and cotton. They all, in varying degrees, have rapidly increasing populations, an Indian problem, need for agrarian reform, economic and political instability stemming from a two-tier society, and very limited internal markets. Because of their similarities and the lack of any "tall poppy" in the group, the climate for economic integration is obviously much better than where great disputations between nations not only tend to divide but to accentuate the difficulties of cooperation. With increased prosperity it is not an unrealistic vision to anticipate complete unity between the members of this one isthmus. Unlike the states of Europe, their histories impel them in this direction, and the benefit of a common language, common institutions and common social and economic problems should surely be a powerful basis to build a union to the greater strength of all of them.

[1]See Postscript, 1971, p. 96.

6

The alternative is not between the status quo and violent revolution. It is between peaceful and violent revolution.

TEODORO MOSCOSO

Problems of Political Evolution

Caudillos: the social revolutions: Christian democrats: the new military "left". The fluctuations of United States policy, and Latin American reactions.

When one considers the diversity of Latin America and the multiplicity of social and economic problems which beset the continent, some of which have been outlined, it is little wonder that there are difficulties in dealing with the problems politically. The task would be difficult even if the two dozen republics were mature democracies of long standing, and if there were several centuries available to deal with the problems by slow evolutionary change. As it is, at the collapse of the Iberian colonial empires in the second decade of the nineteenth century, the regimes that took over control had little or no experience of self-government. They were faced with the acute problems of readjustment and the establishment and recognition of their new nations in the international scene; there were rival factions jostling for power; and there were inevitable frustrations that the change of masters had effected little real change.

In the course of time, at varying stages during the century that followed, there emerged in some of the republics personalities of tremendous influence who put the ship of state on an even keel and drove it forward, perhaps somewhat arbitrarily but at least in a way to subdue divisive dissension and provide a climate for economic progress. Among this number were Portales of Chile,

Fig. 19. *Political Complexion, 1970*

Rosas of Argentina and Batlle y Ordóñez of Uruguay, who in very different ways provided these three countries with a basis for future development. In many other republics, with political dissension overwhelming them, there was the resort to the military *caudillo*. The traditional Latin American dictator installed by a coup d'état and maintained by the armed forces became the "normal" political pattern. In some countries this has continued almost without interruption to the present day. Paraguay, Haiti and Nicaragua have never had a true democratic government, and Stroessner, Duvalier and Somoza are, in effect, dictators for life unless discontented groups find sufficient power to overthrow them. In this century Porfírio Díaz of Mexico, Gómez of Venezuela, Trujillo of the Dominican Republic are other examples of personal rule in which the republics concerned were largely managed as the private estates of these powerful leaders.

In yet another group of republics, dictators have been overthrown and with them the whole social and economic system with which they were identified. Reference has already been made to these three social revolutions in which Cárdenas became the symbol of the new Mexico, Paz Estenssoro of Bolivia and Castro of Cuba.

In an areally small group of states, Jamaica, Trinidad, Barbados, Guyana, the Lesser Antilles, the full emancipation from British colonial rule has come about only in the post-war years, but, as the result of long preparation in democratic institutions, the transition has been a smooth and relatively peaceful one (Fig. 19).

Throughout the last 150 years of the post-independence existence of the republics events in other parts of the world have had a profound influence on their political evolution. Emancipated largely as a result of the turmoil of the Napoleonic wars in their mother countries, their theoretical institutional framework owed much to both the French and the American revolutions; and their survival as independent nations similarly was much dependent on such overseas attitudes as British recognition and the Monroe Doctrine.

It is, however, in this century that economic and political disasters elsewhere have led to widespread consequences in the economic and political history of the republics. The great world economic depression of four decades ago, with its phenomenal contraction of world trade, could not but have a shattering effect on the commodity exports of Latin America. As an example, the exports of Chilean nitrate and copper fell from 1500 million pesos in 1925 to 180 million pesos in 1932. The whole trading and financial structure of their economies collapsed, and with them collapsed government after government, even in the most stable of countries such as Uruguay and Chile. In the latter republic there were no less than eight regimes in eighteen months, the only period of political instability experienced by the republic throughout the seven decades of the twentieth century. It is from this period that so many of the republics determined that a wider base must be found for their economies and active steps were taken to speed the process of industrialisation, disappointing though the results have been.

The influence of the Second World War and the respectability of democratic institutions as enunciated in Roosevelt's four freedoms led to a great dissolution of dictatorial regimes in Latin America and a relaxation of anti-Americanism in the sunshine of Roosevelt's Good Neighbour policy. But as the frustrations of the 1950s and 1960s grew over United States intervention in Guatemala, Cuba and the Dominican Republic, over the restoration of unfavourable terms of trade, over the slow economic growth and the worsening social problems accentuated by rapidly rising populations, the old "remedy" was used again. The *caudillos* came back. One by one, and principally in the giants of Argentina and Brazil, dictatorship again took over. This is the political climate in which this book appears and it is important to take a closer look at the origins, character and prospects of Latin America in the light of these events.

No one would deny that the economic and social problems facing Latin America are so widespread, complex and serious that some massive steps have to be taken, and taken soon, to overcome or at least alleviate the worst of them. There is no doubt that compared with all other continents, and in spite of the problems that those continents also face, Latin America is far less dynamic and far more entrenched in a pattern of status quo than any other. In the post-war period there was a climate of hopeful optimism. There was hope of the incipient industrial revolution which was going to broaden the economic basis of Latin America, to shake its static society out of its conservative lethargy and to give the underprivileged masses some glimpse of the fuller life made possible by twentieth century technology. International aid, the growth of domestic capital, education, a new-found national identity and economic self-determination freeing them from colonial dependence, were all going to revitalise at least the larger and more well-endowed of the republics. It found expression in a variety of ways: the work of the Chilean Development Corporation with its sound economic achievements of providing an energy power base for an expanded industrial structure, the *marcha para o oueste* of Kubitschek to weld Brazil into the great nation everyone has forecast for its destiny, the overthrow of the century-old grip of dictatorship on Venezuela, the birth of the Federation of the West Indies and the emancipation of the *descamisados* by Perón.

In this latter case Frank Owen, in a survey highly critical of the Perón regime finally admits that the dictator "had also conferred upon organised labour a dignity it had never known under the ancient regime. He had given the despised city slum *descamisado* and the tramp farm hand some kind of decent deal at last. The workers had learned to raise their heads, and if some lifted them too high, at least they saw a star in the sky for the first time in their lives."[1]

The last sentence of this quotation aptly describes the promised rebirth of the continent. Yet today, as Latin America stands on the threshold of the last quarter of the twentieth century, the promise seems to have largely faded into the familiar pattern of what John Mander calls "a static society, doomed by the intense conservatism of its social structure, a continent in a state of constant revolution, yet whose revolutions are intended to make sure that nothing changes."[2]

This may appear a harshly cynical and pessimistic assessment of the present situation, but the dragging economic growth of the republics, the perpetuation of lack of confidence of the capitalists in their own country as evidenced by the location of their funds in Europe, the limited impact of the Alliance for Progress, the continued dependence on unsatisfactory terms of trade, the sluggish effects of limited agrarian reform, and the fact that less than one-quarter of the population live under regimes with any fundamentally democratic purpose or system, are facts which certainly do not match the hopes of the last thirty years.

The earlier chapters have outlined some of the social and economic entanglements of the scene, and inevitably there is the dilemma of what political framework provides the best means by which the intermeshed ills may be untangled and a new fabric of a more just, more prosperous and progressively modern society may be woven.

There have been those, and Sımon Bolívar and Haya de la Torre among them, who have seen the salvation in continental unity, in a great United States of Latin America, or perhaps a little less magnificently, in a United States of South America, or of Spanish America. In any one of these concepts there is, of

[1]Owen, Frank., *Perón, His Rise and Fall.* London, 1957, p. 248.
[2]Mander, John, *Static Society: The Paradox of Latin America.* London, 1969.

course, much that is very attractive. In spite of the diversity, perhaps because of the diversity, such a union of 100, 200 or 300 million people in a continent so richly endowed could not but provide itself with a vast accretion of economic strength both absolutely and as a bargaining unit in world trade. The potentialities are enormous, and with its demographic growth, pooled resources, integrated and planned development, the means by which the continent could take a leap forward would be immeasurably increased.

The Central American Common Market and the Latin American Free Trade Area with their limited achievements point the way to what could be realised were this economic cooperation carried to its logical conclusion, but the trade obstacles are still incomparably greater than they were in the countries of the European Economic Community before they founded the European Common Market. And the long haul of that organisation towards political union has scarcely begun.

Despite the advantages of a common language in the Spanish-speaking countries and the common historical, cultural, and colonial inheritance, the attemps at even sub-continental unity in Latin America have always foundered. The Peruvian-Bolivian Confederation, the United Provinces of the River Plate, the Central American federation, the Gran Colombian federation of Ecuador, Colombia and Venezuela, the Federation of the West Indies are the historical debris of these attempts. An entrenched nationalism, frontier disputes, wasteful expenditure on national armies, cruisers and jet fighters, and the senseless economics of duplicated industries on both sides of a common international frontier are all part of the panoply and paraphernalia of separate national identities which outrival Europe, the birth-continent of nationalism.

It is indeed doubtful, to say the least, if the United States would welcome the evolution of a powerful economic and political unit to the south, outnumbering it in population two to one, and confronting its policies with a united and independent voice. As a pliant ally it would have its attractions, but this possibility is more remote than the conjured-up vision of the political union. That this is not mere speculation, it is only necessary to point out the hostility of the United States to the southern bloc of Argentina, Chile, Paraguay and Bolivia adumbrated by Perón in the 1950s. While in theory there must be "strength in unity", there is no doubt that, consciously or unconsciously, the old adage of "divide and rule" has proved realistically useful to the United States in crisis after crisis in the Latin American hemisphere.

While all hope that the regional blocs of LAFTA and of the CACM will do much to strengthen the republics constituting them, it is stating the obvious to say that the future political destiny of the continent will have to be worked out on the three dozen or so national scenes. The most that we can hope for is that influences for good enacted on one stage may spread across the international frontiers and change the individual components of the continent piece by piece. Perhaps in the long run it will be better this way, rather than that a vast political giant, frustrated by the sheer difficulties of government of so many diverse and geographically fragmented peoples, should plunge from one extreme politicalism to its antithesis, dragging its peoples into misery, violence and internal strife and civil war.

If then the future lies in national evolution, the question is under what type of regime and what kind of programme? The usual answer for a century and a half has been that of the military caudillo or junta ruling "for the sake of national unity", in "the preservation of traditional values", "to ensure discipline, law and order". These trite objectives roll off the announcements of each dictatorship installed by a coup d'état, and are euphemisms for the defence of the status quo, the landed interests, the armed forces, the Church's privileged position, and often, quite indirectly, foreign investment. That this "solution" has consistently failed, we have only to survey the present situation. It is precisely because so much national income has been squandered year after year on the national armed forces, because the Church hierarchy for so long has pursued an ostrich-like ultramontane attitude to Latin America's problems, because the landed aristocracy have regarded their tax-exempt control of the rural landscape and its teeming millions as a divinely appointed social system enshrining national stability, and because foreign investment has developed an exploitative, extractive economy in the place of an internally generated expanding development, that the continent is faced with the critical problems of today.

There were those who, having followed for decades Latin America's strivings, felt in the 1940s that there was an almost inevitable progression from this state of affairs, that there were promising signs that the nations of the continent would liberate themselves slowly from this "dictatorship of the right" pattern. Now the process has gone into reverse, and not only have some of the smaller and less developed republics maintained the caudillo leadership, but the Latin American giants of Argentina and Brazil have, since 1964, installed repressive governments dominated by the armed forces. No longer is there, as so often in the past, a guilt complex about this development, whereby promises of more democratic institutions in the near future gave a temporary complexion to the junta's assumption of power. In Brazil a constitutional permanence of the dictatorship has been fastened upon the nation, in Argentina the restoration of democracy is equally remote and a military regime is in control for an explicitly indefinite period.[1]

Disapproval by the United States and by other foreign governments often resulted in the non-recognition of those regimes installed by military force and maintaining an arbitrary control over their nations' destinies. In general this ostracism has had little real effect, and the implementation and impact of policies of non-recognition are variable. Indeed non-recognition may do much to entrench such regimes in popular support of a defensive nationalism against outside interference. This is not to say that the continuance of such regimes should be strengthened by generous economic support or by active cooperation with their policies of static conventionalism. Still less is it necessary, or even wise politically, to confer honours upon dictators as occurred in the case of President Eisenhower's bestowal of the United States Legion of Merit on the dictator of Venezuela, Pérez Jiménez, in 1954 or the telegram of congratulation sent by the U.S. ambassador to the military leaders of Brazil in the 1964 coup.

Unfortunately the attractions of dictatorial control of economic affairs, orthodox commercial transactions and deflationary policies, often appeal to foreign financiers who judge a nation by statistical norms and the outlook for foreign commercial companies and not by the implementation of basic reforms to improve the economic and social welfare of the population as a whole.

A recent article, "Brazil, The Turn of the Tide", gives this viewpoint.[2] It begins "The Brazilian economy has made impressive progress so far this year" and ends "If no basic alterations are made to current policies, the (country's economic) prospects now seem brighter than at any time since 1945". The question which immediately arises is "bright for whom?" Certainly not for the two-thirds of the 95 million who live outside the economy, doing nothing more than barely subsisting, certainly not for the desperate inhabitants of the North-east described by Monsignor Helder Cámara, Archbishop of Olinda-Recife as "one of the most under-developed areas in the world where the people are poorer than the people of India."

[1]The latest proposal is that power will be handed over to a democratically elected government on 12 October 1973. See Postscript, 1971, p. 89.

[2]"Brazil. The Turn of the Tide." *Bolsa Review*. Vol. 3, No. 35, Nov. 1969, pp. 674-79.

To quote the Archbishop again:

> Out of 90 million Brazilians, 45 million haven't even 36 new cruzeiros (about 7 Australian dollars) a month to make a pretence of a living. Only 22 out of every 100 Brazilians have work. Out of every 100 families living in Brazil, 70 do not even receive the minimum wage. Of 1000 million acres which represents the total of all the 3,800,000 properties registered in Brazil, almost half belong to one per cent of the owners.
>
> Can one talk of "order" when faced with that picture? Is maintaining that situation to maintain order or to perpetuate disorder and injustice, the seeds of hatred?[1]

If the Brazilian picture of political repression, censorship, and military oppression was the only one in the continent, it would be serious in itself, but a similar fate holds Argentina, Paraguay, Nicaragua, Haiti and Panama in the grip of armed overlords whose main objective is to see that nothing changes in the basic structure of their societies.

With a far less heavy burden of problems than Brazil, Argentina has always lived in the shadow of military rule, but since 1955 the army has been determined that the influence of the millions of voters who still support Peronist policies must never be exerted on the government. In the last decade the two constitutionally elected Presidents, Frondizi and Illia, have been deposed, and the military leaders, headed first by Ongañia, then by Levingston and now by Lanusse have clamped once more the traditional dictatorship of the right on Argentina.[2]

It is not surprising, therefore, that so many Latin Americans despairing of this repetitive pattern of oppression, and the continuing increase of misery, hunger and neglect, have turned to violent revolution as the only means of breaking into the circle and liberating the energy and wealth of the continent. As indicated in an earlier chapter there have been three such revolutions in which the entrenched system of latifundia, monopolistic investment and a caste society has been overthrown—Mexico, Bolivia

[1]*Seeking Justice and Peace*. Archbishop Helder Cámara, reported in the *New Christian* 20 March 1969.

[2]President Ongañia was deposed in June 1970 as a result of a coup d'etat by the armed forces. The new President, General Roberto Levingston announced his intention to return the country to constitutional rule, but also to give the armed forces greater participation in the Government. By March 1971 Levingston had reaped the reward of this policy—for attempting to dismiss the Commander-in-Chief of the army, General Alejandro Lanusse, he found himself overthrown and Lanusse installed as President.

and Cuba. Each is different because the republics are so different from each other and because external events have influenced their evolutions at different periods of world history. All have, by their violent nature, involved bloodshed, destruction and dispossession, and major social upheaval. All have, however, unified the population in immeasurably increased self-respect, a massive urge for education, and an identification of the people with the land. Utopia has not been reached, but their leaders would be the first to stress that the revolutions have scarcely begun. Luis Echeverría the new President of Mexico, the earliest of the revolutionary republics, in his first statement on being chosen as presidential candidate insisted "the Mexican Revolution isn't over yet", and that his beliefs were based on *"arriba y adelante"*—ahead and forward.

Despite their difficulties, often in the face of external opposition, particularly exemplified in the United States' attitudes to Mexico and Cuba, their achievements must attract the underprivileged and hungry masses of the other republics. Literally they have nothing to lose, and apparently much to gain. There is scarcely a republic which is not affected by a movement with much popular support to liberate their country from the economic, political and social stagnation which has been endemic as long as can be remembered. It has found various expressions such as the *violencia* which has plagued Colombia ever since the death of Gaitán, the introduced guerilla movements of Venezuela and Bolivia, the urban revolution of the Argentinian and Brazilian cities with street battles, burnings, sabotage and kidnappings, the well-organised Tupumaro guerilla movement of Montevideo, and the abortive attempts to free Haiti from its medieval bondage. In many areas it is probably only the lack of a leader which has saved many countries from social revolutions comparable with that of Cuba. Haiti, Jamaica and North-eastern Brazil certainly have sufficient inflammable material in rural poverty only to need organising in direct and massive confrontation of the status quo. Once "the oppressed classes are aware that some other way of life is possible and their ambitions are stirred, from then on revolt . . . becomes largely a matter of the appearance of leaders".[1] In most areas, however, the army stands poised to crush such revolutions. Where they have failed to do so, as in Mexico and Cuba, the new regimes have had to face military intervention or economic blockade by the United States, usually in defence of their commercial interests. Only in Bolivia, largely as a result of

[1]Simpson, E. N. *The Ejido, Mexico's Way Out*. Chapel Hill, 1937, p. 44.

wise advice from its ambassador did the United States cooperate with the great revolutionary surge to establish the nation on a more just and progressive path of emancipation.[1]

Perhaps it is more surprising that there are so many millions who have faith in a democratic evolutionary political solution, but the examples of the Western democratic nations in which prosperity, social justice and increased standards of living have been won by parliamentary means have had a profound effect on many of the more intelligent and educated in Latin America. I do not refer to the conventional parties largely committed to the preservation of the present iniquitous pattern, for these are little better than the military dictatorships of the right with whom they frequently collaborate, but to those movements that aim for "revolution in freedom" as the Alliance for Progress described its purpose.

> The traditional parties with their various names—Radicals, Conservatives, Colorados, Blancos—are usually little but highly personalised cliques with few and shallow roots in the countryside . . . representative institutions are tarnished by over a century of massive corruption, manipulation, peculation, and fraud.[2]

Apart from the parties formed to defend the social revolutions, the *Partido Revolucionario Institucional* (PRI) of Mexico, the *Movimiento Nacional Revolucionario* (MNR) of Bolivia and Castro's Communist party of Cuba, the most significant parties committed to radical reform are the *Acción Democratica* (AD) and Social Christian parties (COPEI) of Venezuela, which have falteringly endeavoured to salvage that country from its dictatorial heritage, and the Christian Democratic party and "Popular Front" socialist coalition of the *Frente de Acción Popular* (FRAP) in Chile.[3]

In spite of its relatively peaceful constitutional evolution since independence in the early nineteenth century, Chile has all the characteristics of the Latin American malaise—gross inequalities of income distribution, malnutrition, high infant mortality, inadequate housing and education, inflation, agricultural decline, economic stagnation, mono-metal dependence, and foreign in-

[1]One U.S. writer suggests that as the U.S. embassy in La Paz is not "a particularly delectable plum for amateurs in search of a diplomatic post" the conduct of U.S. relations with Bolivia has been in the hands of career diplomats, who have had an active sympathy for the aims the Bolivian social revolution has been attempting to achieve (Alexander p. 259).

[2]Finer, S. E. "The Argentine Trouble", in *Encounter,* Sept. 1965, p. 60.

[3]Elected to office under Salvador Allende in October 1970.

debtedness. A succession of constitutionally elected governments—Conservative, Radical and Nationalist—have failed to make sufficiently rapid and fundamental changes to cope with its problems. In 1964 the Chilean people discarded the traditional parties and were given a choice between two revolutionary programmes, a Socialist-Communist solution which frankly admitted that it saw little possibility of implementing its reforms without arbitrary methods, and a new Christian Democratic solution of "a revolution in liberty". Choosing the latter, the Chilean experiment became the focus of attention throughout the Latin American continent. Perhaps too much was expected of President Frei's six-year period to transform the Chilean scene, "to demolish the structure of existing society and build a new one", but there were many who saw it as Chile's last, best hope.[1]

That hope, however, was a forlorn one. Despite unprecedented parliamentary support and a surge of popular optimism, the unity of the Christian Democratic party was broken into more progressive and more conservative groups, and the party's urge towards a revolution in liberty was overwhelmed by the day-to-day problems of administration.

The traditional parties of Left and Right regained much of their strength, and in the 1970 presidential election, Frei's hoped-for successor Radomiro Tomic was defeated. So also was the former President Alessandri, the candidate of the status quo. Salvador Allende, leader of the Popular Front coalition of socialist and communist parties, in quite typical Chilean adherence to democracy, became the new President. Most significant was the fact that the combined votes of the reform candidates Tomic and Allende outnumbered the conservative forces almost two to one. Thus, just as Chile was the first Latin American republic to try a Christian Democratic solution for its chronic ills, so it became the first such republic, in free elections, to risk a socialist solution.

What else remains? Strangely a new phenomenon for Latin America has made its appearance—military dictatorship of the left. There are those who have compared it with Nasser's Egyptian revolution or Argentina's Peronismo. Certainly in both there were threads of nationalism and of socialism, but it is deceptive to indulge in comparisons of two different historical periods. Instead, a new movement has been born, of young military men, who are conscious of the vast impulse needed to build a new Latin America. Rejecting both the path of violent revolution and the frustrating circle of traditional political inability "to get things moving",

[1]Leonard Gross *The Last, Best Hope: Eduardo Frei and Chilean Democracy*. New York, 1967.

they see their function to create national revolutions by cutting through the web of opposition by fundamental and vigorous reforms. This completely new role of the military promoting radical social change is seen at its best in Peru. Indeed its policy has been dubbed *peruanismo*.[1] This policy aims to free the Peruvian economy from foreign control and from the vested interests of the Peruvian upper classes. To do this it has set out to reform the whole social and economic structure of Peru, to nationalise the water resources and the transport network, to streamline the governmental bureaucracy, to reconstruct the taxation system and to introduce a radical agrarian reform programme, second only to Cuba's in its magnitude and widespread objectives. In fact the present Peruvian government is largely engaged in carrying out the reforms originally suggested by APRA forty years ago.

In many ways the slant given to the Bolivian Revolution by the 1964 military overthrow of Paz Estenssoro reflects this left nationalist movement. It is not without interest that, on the death of its leader, General Barrientos, in April 1969, the peasant masses hoped that General Ovando, the Commander-in-Chief of the armed forces, would succeed him. There was in fact an interlude of five months, during which time President Siles, a civilian, held the office; but the fact that the natural coalition was between the army and the rural population indicates the taking over of the social revolution by a regime of the military left, and the new President has made several policy statements much in line with similar declarations of the new Peruvian leaders. It is significant that the portfolios in the new Bolivian cabinet headed by army men are the Interior, Economy, Mines and Petroleum, Public Works and Rural Affairs.

Unlike military regimes of the right the new Peruvian government does not take a partisan approach in international relations, but maintains contact with East and West, and has recently entered into contracts with Rumania and Hungary and received credits from Poland and Czechoslovakia, while technical help is being received from nations as diverse as West Germany, France, Japan, Britain and the Soviet Union. Indeed as long as Peru's national resources do not pass out of its control, the help of foreign capital in its task of emancipating Peru is welcomed. In line with regaining economic control, the foreign-owned telephone and telegraph companies have been brought into public ownership,

[1]D. J. R. "Peruanismo—the new revolution", *Bolsa Review*, Vol. 3, No. 35, November 1969, pp. 685-7.

and the expropriation of the property of the International Petroleum Company, a subsidiary of Standard Oil of New Jersey, can be compared only with similar actions by the Cuban revolutionary regime. Although this action by Peru led to heated discussion in the U.S. press and a torrent of threats by members of Congress, the U.S. government reacted relatively calmly. In fact the United States is faced with a most unusual phenomenon in a military-supported nationalist and socialist approach to Latin American problems. It is almost impossible to attribute developments in Peru to a deep-seated, nefarious, Communist plot as it was easy to do in Guatemala in 1954, British Guiana in 1953 and 1962, the Dominican Republic in 1965, and Brazil in 1964.

If this active participation by the armed forces in carrying forward the social revolution that Latin America so desperately needs becomes contagious, a new fluidity will be introduced into the possibilities of dynamic transformation of the stagnant socio-economic scene. It will be the second of the great institutional forces, hitherto in alliance with the status quo, which have seen the necessity for a radical change. The first such volteface was made by the other great Latin American institution, the Church. Indeed it is from many notable leaders of religious thought that a new spirit of hope has shone in the darkest recesses of the continent. Just as, in the days of the birth of political independence five generations back many a pastor was in the forefront of movements for emancipation from Spain, so today the poor and oppressed have been rallied in the knowledge that their spiritual leaders cared for their physical suffering and socio-economic distress. What more convincing proof that this is not mere polemics can be found than the petition signed by five million workers and peasants nominating Monsignor Helder Cámara for the 1970 Nobel Peace Prize? In this plea the petitioners say that the priest "symbolises for us the struggle for the liberation of man and of the Latin Americans, without which there can be neither peace, nor justice, nor progress."

Not all sectors of the Latin American church are in the forefront of progress as is Archbishop Helder Cámara, for many of the oligarchies of the church in the more ultramontane republics bitterly oppose change, but they appear to be diminishing in number, and Pope Paul's call in Bogotá for greater social and economic justice further weakened their effectiveness.

It is perhaps symptomatic of the forgotten continent that everyone has heard of Gandhi and Martin Luther King, but few of Helder Cámara; yet his mission of non-violent revolution is the same as theirs, "to seek the change which is so urgently required by the force of ideas and justice, and by democratic methods."[1]

This is the great political problem of Latin America—to right the great social and economic ills which continue to plague the lives of the overwhelming majority of its citizens, to do it in the least violent way, and yet to do it quickly and with massive impact before half a billion, having tried every non-violent path, choose the only alternative in a desperate bid for liberation.

As so often in the past, the influence of the United States is crucial. It is quite obvious that, for its own security and peace of mind, a stable, happy, prosperous and democratic society in the vast continent to the south is a necessity and an objective to be striven for. Yet, while all would agree with the need, the policies of the United States government and of the big corporations and investment sources influenced by it have been by no means consistent or well-devised to achieve these ends.

There has been, in fact, considerable vacillation and uncertainty as to how to deal with the nations south of the Río Grande. At first, there came the Monroe Doctrine, which in essence is a warning notice of "no trespassers" to the rest of the world. It is a policy of paternal protection for the Western, American, hemisphere, of non-interference by Europe in particular, which, for centuries, of course was the only area of the world from which interference was likely to come. In the context of the last half of the twentieth century, of power politics by the world's two super powers, it is the American sphere of influence, where Russia cynically gives the United States a free hand, just as the United States, equally cynically, gives Russia a free hand in Eastern Europe. The two case examples of the Dominican Republic in 1965 and of Czechoslovakia in 1968 illustrate this mutual partition of spheres of influence perfectly. Just as the United States intervened in the Dominican Republic from a panic-stricken fear of another Communist state in the American sphere of influence, so Russia intervened in Czechoslovakia from a panic-stricken fear of the development of a capitalist "Western" state in the Russian sphere. In parallel ways the armies of the satellites of the two powers were involved to give an aura of areal solidarity, the Warsaw Pact nations on the one hand, the military dictatorial regimes of Brazil and Central America on the other. There are other similarities, but the significance of the exclusive position of the United States relative to the other American continent has

[1]Monsignor Helder Cámara's own words in an interview with Alexander Craig "Reform or Revolution", *New Christian*, 11 July 1968, p. 16.

been made. Yet in spite of the early establishment of this position, the United States for a long time largely ignored the society and economy of Latin America, so preoccupied was it with its own internal development and expanding nationhood; and the southern continent received much more investment in money, men and materials from Europe. It is in this period that Argentina in particular became a part of Britain's economic empire.

In the twentieth century, following the consolidation of the United States' economic strength, and the increasing depletion of many of its natural resources, Latin America became the focus of growing American investment in mineral exploitation (including petroleum), tropical agricultural plantations and the infrastructure of electric power and telecommunications. Venezuela, Cuba, Brazil and Chile in particular were the early investment areas, but more recently Argentina, Colombia, Mexico, Panama and Peru have received much United States external finance. The economic fortunes of the Latin American republics have thus become of direct concern to the American investors and through them to the United States government. By far the major area of concern is the Caribbean, and proportionately no country came in the same group as Venezuela and Cuba, the latter having more United States capital invested in it than did Brazil or Mexico (Fig. 18).

Contemporaneous with this financial involvement came the corollary of a growing solicitude that the regimes in the countries involved should provide stable political conditions to enable the capital to yield its maximum undisturbed dividends. Where instability or political, social or economic unrest threatened, the United States directly intervened, militarily occupied the countries concerned and literally ran the government. In Cuba, the most valued area, the right of direct interference in this fashion was even enshrined in a formal treaty obligation, known as the Platt amendment, but in the first thirty years of this century the United States was quite overtly in political control of the Dominican Republic, Haiti, Nicaragua and Cuba for most of the time. This era of the "big stick" is the one which has given the United States the notoriety of Yankee imperialism throughout the continent—a sobriquet which has been hard for it to live down.

The efforts of Franklin Roosevelt's "Good Neighbour Policy" and of John Kennedy's "Alliance for Progress" were directed towards infusing a completely new philosophy into the relations between the United States and Latin America. In place of intervention and force, the aims of both were social, economic and political reform towards the creation of democratic communities.

In the first phase of this policy reversal, for twenty years (1934-54) there was no wielding of the big stick, and fragile democratic governments were born where none had ever existed before. In the second it was declared that there must be "a vast new effort unparalleled in magnitude and nobility of purpose, to satisfy the basic needs of the American people for homes, work and land, health and schools" and, provided the Latin Americans redirected their energies into social and economic change the United States would provide "resources of a size and magnitude to make this bold plan a success" and so achieve a "revolution in freedom".

In the intervening period, especially under Dulles' foreign policy, Latin America was once again almost forgotten with the United States' involvement in Asia. Indeed an extension of Dulles' holy war on communism saw in Guatemala once again the intervention of the United States in the overthrow of a government which had dared to institute land reforms against the vested interests of the United Fruit Company. Similarly, there was support of the dictators of Cuba, the Dominican Republic and Venezuela —Batista, Trujillo and Pérez Jiménez—for the "stability" of their governments.

Largely as a result of the unenlightened handling of the Cuba Revolution, in contrast to the wisdom shown in the Bolivian experience, the relationships between Latin America and the United States became inextricably entangled in the world ideological struggle between the United States and the U.S.S.R. Cuba became a base for violent guerilla activity in many parts of the continent, and the United States through the Central Intelligence Agency (C.I.A.) developed an opposing campaign of counter-insurgency units.

Of far greater importance to Latin Americans, than the desultory skirmishes in Venezuela and Bolivia, was the United States invasion of the Dominican Republic and its continued support for the Brazilian military dictatorship since 1964. Once again the pattern of military intervention had been resumed, and the identification of the great northern power with reactionary and repressive regimes had been re-established.

The belief of many Latin Americans is that the vested interests of the United States capital in their continent are so strong that, in the final analysis, they control policy. Moreover, they feel that the policy has consistently opposed social revolution and supported reactionary regimes of various vintages. Even more, there has been the tendency to suspect any government with a socialist component to be the seat of communist subversion of the hemisphere. Too often, therefore, have reactionary regimes been installed by connivance or supported as "stable", and equally often have liberal and progressive forces been stifled and driven into an anti-Americanism which the United States public finds difficult to understand. It is only in this way that the violent reactions of Latin American crowds to Vice-President Nixon in 1958, and Nelson Rockefeller in 1969 can be understood. Yet, when a different philosophy was in the ascendant the adulation of Vice-President Wallace in 1940 and of President Kennedy in 1962 was contrastingly impressive.

There is no doubt that the United States is hypersensitive about developments in Latin America, and adopts a two-standards policy in its relationships there and elsewhere. There are scores of examples of the contrast, the reaction to Panama's nationalism over the Canal in 1963 compared with that to Egypt's over the Suez Canal in 1956; the acceptance of a "third world" policy of India but opposition to any suggestion of it in Brazil; the acquiescence in vacating the Libyan United States bases but the agressive determination to hold Guatánamo in Cuba; the friendly visits to and exchanges with communist Romania and China and the ostracism and blockade of communist Cuba.

Mr William D. Rogers, an expert of immense Latin American experience, sums up the Latin American reaction to United States policy quite succinctly "the United States is really only interested in keeping Latin America quiet—that Eurocentrism, a preoccupation with world communism and Mr Monroe's sphere of influence syndrome are the realities of United States ruling in the hemisphere."[1]

From this apparent attitude there is born in Latin America a certain despondency and cynicism that they can really never be masters in their own houses. In spite of, perhaps because of, hemispheric cooperation, the southern governments appear to be mere echoes of the northern giant, and only Mexico, and to a smaller extent Chile and Uruguay, express a continuous individuality—a difficult attitude to adopt when "the overwhelming power of the United States takes on such awesome meaning in time of crisis."[2]

There are signs that very slowly the United States is becoming less excited and dogmatic over Latin American developments, that it is prepared to give more latitude to a wider variety of political solutions in Latin America and to concede a greater

[1]Rogers, William D. "The United States and Latin America" in C. Véliz (ed.) *Latin America and the Caribbean. A Handbook*. London, 1968, p. 429.
[2]Ibid p. 431.

measure of responsibility for the Latin Americans to work out their own salvation in their own way. The example of Mexico would seem to indicate that by methods other than a Westminster or Washington type parliamentary system much social, economic and political progress can be achieved. There is no reason, with the passage of time, that Cuba should not be accommodated smoothly within the continent as Yugoslavia is within Europe. Teodoro Moscoso, the first United States coordinator for the Alliance for Progress declared that "no nation can save another nation". Painfully and in a most costly manner the United States has learned this lesson in Vietnam. Is it too much to hope that in a much less dramatic way the Latin Americans may be given the opportunity to save themselves?

Postscript, 1971

The dictators and their opposition: the Uruguayan Tupumaros: Chile's socialist revolution: Peru and Bolivia, parallel but different: aspects of national economic independence: the CACM: Mexico's continuing struggle.

All the problems outlined in the preceding pages are enacted on a great variety of national stages, large and small. Sometimes significant parts of the scenery are changed; often the characters who play the drama are replaced by others very different in their approach to the problems confronting them.

It is not easy to follow the simultaneous performances on so many parts of the Latin American stage, but major developments are better understood if some assessment is made of trends and movements as this book goes to press. This, then, is the objective of this postscript, not to be an epilogue, but rather a prologue to the events as they unfold in the days ahead, on the other side of the Pacific.

In mid-1971, the strongly entrenched military dictatorships of the right maintain their grip on almost half the area's population. Nowhere is the contrast between the apparent economic progress of a country and the real situation of its people more startling than in Brazil. The plight of the ordinary people reveals the chronic ills about which a repressive dictatorship cares little. Nor is this true only of the depressed and over-populated areas of this vast nation, for in highly developed São Paulo city, infant mortality remains at sixty deaths per thousand births; and 44 per cent of all men and women of working age are unemployed. The minimum salary there and in Rio de Janeiro is about one-quarter of that needed to ensure an adequate standard of living, and indications are that real incomes are falling rather than increasing. It is guesswork to estimate how long the discontent will be contained, but it is not impossible that the lower ranks of the armed forces might provide the catalyst to explode the situation.

Brazil for so long has had a democratic tradition that not all the generals believe in their divine right to rule indefinitely, and one such, Afonso Albuquerque Lima, in April pleaded for "an immediate return to full constitutional rule". Unfortunately, however, the Brazilian War College first established in 1948 for purely military functions, now appears to be the fundamental source and laboratory in which the policies of the present dictatorship are worked out. There is, therefore, a vested interest in the continued political involvement of the military leaders.

Far less assured is the confidence of the military government in Argentina, and few are more disillusioned with that country's economic stagnation than the junta at present in control. The country is divided politically, as much now as it has been since the overthrow of Perón in 1955. The fundamental reason for this long period of instability is the refusal of the military to accept peronismo as a political reality. It is, therefore, welcome that President Lanusse now appears to realise that the peronistas must be participants in any future elected government, although this by no means must involve the physical return of Perón from Spain. The persistent groundswell of popular nostalgia for the more egalitarian and social-oriented policies associated with *justicialismo* (which was how Perón described them) is the fundamental fact of life which has to be accommodated in any future democratic framework in Argentina. Although leaders such as Lanusse now recognise this, there are many hard core personnel in the armed forces who do not, and the struggle between these opposing viewpoints is likely to prolong Argentina's political and socio-economic instability for a long time.

The dictatorships in the smaller countries maintain their nationalistic obscurantism, often despite what might have seemed to be important events within their borders. The death of "Papa Doc" Duvalier led to no significant change, the titular succession going to Jean-Claude Duvalier and the real power probably to his sister Marie-Denise.

Reactions to the removal of long-established dictators do not, however, always occur immediately. In the case of Haiti's neighbour, the Dominican Republic, there was a considerable lapse of time between the assassination of Trujillo and the replacement of the dictatorship by a more democratic regime. Similarly, Haitian emigré opposition will need time to organise and assess the methods most likely to rid their country of the Duvalier stranglehold. After all, the Caribbean has for long had a persistent example in the Nicaraguan Somozas of a family skilful in the manipulation of power, and 1971 was no exception to its continuance. Fearing the success of the Social Democrats and other left-wing groups if free elections were held, such a contest was conveniently postponed to 1974.

The "fictitious peace" of Paraguay, for so long based on an alliance of all the traditional forces of the status quo, was, in 1971, vehemently attacked by the bishops of the country. Their denunciation of the Stroessner regime's corruption, persecution of its opponents and lack of land reform gave hope to many Paraguayans, both within and outside its borders. That the Church was courageous enough to see and work for a better future in South America's most deep-rooted dictatorship, was certainly a breakthrough. On the whole many of the national hierarchies of the Church are conservative in their approach to change, and the stand of the Paraguayan Church is, therefore, all the more impressive.

In the north of the continent, the Colombian Church, without doubt the most reactionary in Latin America, in March, similarly abandoned its alignment with the status quo and called on the government to implement widespread social and economic reforms for a "population which finds itself in a state of misery or subject to the anguish of uncertainty or spurred by the hope of progress". Underlining the mal-distribution of wealth and property as the main cause of Colombia's underdevelopment and "massive unemployment which is our most acute social problem", the bishops called for increased provision of housing and education and more democratic industrial management.

It is not only the dictatorships, however, that have to cope with determined and deep-seated opposition, for in South America's most democratic state, Uruguay, the usually placid stream of political life has been thrown into turmoil by the activities of the Tupumaros, as the urban guerillas of Montevideo style themselves. For generations all Uruguayans have been either Blancos or Colorados, and until 1958 the latter were instrumental in producing a steady current of progressive legislation which transformed Uruguay into the continent's first welfare state. Between 1958 and 1966 the National Party (Blancos) were in power. The return of the Colorados, particularly since Pacheco succeeded to the presidency in 1967 (on the death of President Gestido) has been characterised by increasing instability. The causes are closely linked to an economic situation characterised by unfavourable terms of trade for Uruguayan pastoral production and resultant inflation, high unemployment and a top-heavy governmental bureaucratic structure. Politically, moreover, progressive forces within the country feel that Uruguay has not only run out of momentum in social advancement, but that the more dynamic programmes of countries such as Chile and Peru accentuate the extent to which Uruguay now lags behind.

During 1971 the Tupumaros have revealed themselves not only as the most efficiently organised urban guerillas in the continent, but the spearhead of a considerable popular movement of criticism and attack upon the forces of the status quo. This has developed into a broad left-wing front (*Frente Amplio de Izquierda*) which threatens to provide a real challenge to the conventional parties, which, in the face of the challenge, are fragmenting and recombining in confusing rapidity—so much so that many have doubts if the November presidential elections will take place. Even more dramatically, the fear has been expressed that Brazil might intervene to prevent a left-wing take-over of power on its southern borders.

Although Montevideo's overgrown size in relation to the population distribution in Uruguay gives it a large concentration of political power, it is quite possible that the more conservative rural areas with the larger number of voters will effectively prevent the presidential contest producing a radical revolutionary change. Whether the capital's discontented urban masses would peacefully accept such rural control is highly doubtful; and Uruguay's political future is now more uncertain than at any time in this century.

No single political development in 1971, however, has had more significant national and international impact than the progressive implementation of socialist policies carried out by Chile's new government. As so often in the past, Chile has been in the forefront of political development, and its experimentation with radical methodology since 1938 (when it elected one of the world's first Popular Front governments) has placed it in a unique category. Equally significant has been the adherence to democratic norms and the peaceful transference of power from one elected government to another. There are those, on right and left, who would try to prevent these smooth transitions and the Allende government has had to be particularly vigilant in this respect in view of its sweeping reformist policies in relation to property, long-established vested interests and the whole social hierarchical system.

By late 1971, however, the new administration had considerably consolidated its position in the country. Municipal elections in April had indicated that its popularity had increased to include more than half the electorate. For many of its legislative measures it had secured the support of the Christian Democrats, still the largest party in Congress; and the nationalisation of the large copper mines had evoked a considerable emotional identification of the Chilean people with their national emancipation. This is exemplified by the unanimous vote of Congress to approve the measure, and the parallel drawn between the day of nationalisation and the country's day of political independence.

Among the Government's most notable achievements to date have been a considerable increase in industrial production, a continuous fall in unemployment and a long-striven-for decline in inflationary pressures, although there are undoubtedly still severe financial problems to be faced. Foremost among these is the movement of capital overseas and increased imports caused by industrial expansion. A sweeping absorption of large sectors of industry and banking into national ownership has provided the basis for the implementation and building of a socialist economy. The Government seems well aware that the six year term of the Chilean presidency is a short period in which to carry through a programme of permanent radical transformation. The vigour and breadth of the first year of its legislative programme bear a close resemblance to the equally comprehensive series of measures swiftly enacted by Britain's post-war Labour government of 1945.

Of special interest has been the reaction of the United States government to these developments. The election of President Allende clearly came as a shock to the Nixon administration, and there were some external manifestations of the latter's disapproval, such as the cancellation of the visit of the aircraft-carrier *Enterprise*, the openly unfriendly attitude to Chile's representative at the Alliance for Progress meeting in Washington, and a similarly critical reaction by President Nixon to the Allende government in his February review of foreign policy. More significant and welcome, however, has been the lack of really hostile action, even against the take-over of the major United States financial interests in Chile, and in particular those involved in the operation of the large copper mines. There would indeed appear to be real hope that the United States has at last recognised the truth of President Kennedy's assessment of Latin America: "Those who make peaceful revolution impossible will make violent revolution inevitable".

Equally welcome has been the reaction of Argentina to events west of the Andes. The Declaration of Salta signed by Allende and Lanusse in July almost solely concerns itself with the need to modernise their countries' social and economic structures. So often in the past such declarations have been preoccupied with political condemnations of subversion and terrorism and the identification of ideological frontiers and have had no real meaning in the lives and welfare of the peoples concerned.

This new Argentine position is, of course, diametrically different from the conventional Brazilian doctrine of antagonism to political change. In fact Lanusse's apparent recognition of the strength and broad-based popular support for the regimes in power in Chile, Bolivia and Peru, and the advantage to Argentina of cooperation with them might be a major break-through in the alignment of a great part of South America, from Iquitos to Cape Horn, into broadly similar social and economic objectives to improve their peoples' lot. That the political systems under which these objectives are pursued might differ in relation to each republic's political evolution would matter little provided the socio-economic results were obtained. There will have to be, however, a considerable change of heart in Argentina's military hierarchy if Lanusse's apparent international alignment is translated into effective internal policy change.

The method of Bolivia "to build socialism" in that poverty-stricken land appears to be increasingly motivated from its new People's Assembly. The mining unions, which since the 1952 social revolution have been the most powerful political bloc, have taken over control of the Assembly, and their leader, Juan Lechín, has been elected its head. The economic base of the country dependent almost entirely upon high prices for tin in the world market, is, however, still precarious. Until the eastern half of the country provides a more diversified balance to the nation's economy, the crisis between political desirability and economic feasibility will continue to be more acute than in any other South American republic. What is particularly interesting in Bolivia is the location of political power in the trade unions rather than in the factions-riven doctrinaire political parties. Above all, the miners show no readiness to accept orders from the professional politicians, which emphasises once again the grass-roots nature of the Bolivian Revolution. The extent to which the presidential rule of Tórrez can accommodate itself to the influence and power of the Assembly is the unknown factor in Bolivia's immediate political future.

At mid-1971 the continuance of the radical orientation of the military government of Peru would appear to be in the balance. This is hardly surprising in view of the long-established dictatorship of the right which has dominated Peruvian politics throughout history. The strength of Peru's landed oligarchy is still significant and is still represented in military circles. However the Velasco government continues to pursue its own policies of social change, dramatic in intensity for the Peruvian political scene. These include the creation of an organisation to consolidate and increase civilian support for the social and economic measures of the Government. The reliance of Peruvian development for so long on foreign investment is a difficult problem to resolve. To pursue a policy of uncompromising economic nationalism immediately would lead to disaster. The aim, therefore, is to initiate a transition which will liberate the economy gradually from its colonial dependence and at the same time maintain the interest of the foreign investor. This is no easy course to follow and it will dominate Peruvian economics and politics for years to come.

Although the parallel but different policies of Chile, Bolivia and Peru are inevitably conditioned by the very different political evolution and economic conditions of the three republics, there is an interesting and significant common attitude to international relations. No longer is there acceptance of the United States-imposed ostracism of the ideologically-opposed nations of the world. Chile, of course, led the way with the resumption of diplomatic relations with Cuba and China, but there has also been a resurgence of economic contacts between all three Andean republics and eastern European nations.

In this connection it is paradoxical that President Nixon, who in February criticised Chile's re-establishment of relations with China, should in July indicate that the United States was embarking on a similar course. This is as hard to understand as the paradox between the United States' economic policies towards Eastern Europe whereby Romania, Poland and Yugoslavia have been awarded "most favoured nation" treatment, and its continued economic blockade of its neighbour Cuba.

There has, in fact, been a general liberalisation of contacts between most parts of Latin America and the rest of the world, and a considerable break-down in the routine association of the continent with North America and Western Europe only. The most sensitive area in this connection is Cuba. No country outside the Americas (and Canada, Jamaica and Mexico within the Americas) has accepted advice from the United States to uphold that country's economic blockade of Cuba. Britain and Spain in particular, and of course Russia, China and Eastern Europe, have continued to trade quite profitably with the island. In 1971 Cuba also became a major recipient of Swedish foreign aid in diverse fields of education, dairy products, industrialisation, transport equipment such as bulldozers and the building of ships. Even Australia risked the ire of the United States in the supply of sugar harvesting machinery.

Apart, however, from these specific economic developments, the most common policy trend evident in 1971 is what the Bank of London and South America, through its chairman, described as the "latest wave of nationalism sweeping Latin America". This is not an emotional, political reaction in any jingoistic sense, but a common assertion to defend the interests of Latin America vis-a-vis the rich and powerful nations of the developed world. In all aspects where the relationships of Latin America with those nations are unequal, there is widespread and increasing action to strive towards greater equality. This action is not limited to the more democratic countries, but stems from unexpected sources, such as Brazil's triple confrontation with the United States over issues as far apart as exports of soluble coffee, the 200-mile offshore limit and freight monopolies. Similarly, Colombia, which in 1971 moved towards more and more conservative policies, including the abandonment of its feeble agrarian reform programme,[1] supported the other four countries of the Andean group of LAFTA in the Lima Agreement establishing maximum limits to foreign investment in such matters as the percentage of control and the rate of dividends.

Mention has already been made of the nationalisation of United States' copper mines in Chile. A similar step in May restored to Bolivia the control of its zinc and lead production; while three months earlier Guyana took over Alcan's bauxite mines, which provide 85 per cent of that country's dollar earnings from bauxite and alumina. Comprehensive legislation is being enacted in Venezuela to nationalise the natural gas industry, the unexploited oil concessions of foreign companies, and ultimately all their properties when the used concessions expire in 1983.

These moves against North American-owned assets continue the nationalisation policies of the Velasco government of Peru in the seizure of sugar lands and the oil properties of the International Petroleum Company in 1969. They reflect the widespread determination of Latin Americans that foreign aid must not involve foreign control and that the exploitation of their resources will provide the financial means to provide a more favourable social environment for their underprivileged peoples.

The reaction of the involved North American interests to these events has been relatively mild, although the extent of the compensation offered may in some cases provoke reprisals or threats of counter-measures. This is most likely in respect of the Chilean copper mines on account of the large investment involved (Fig. 18) and the gap which undoubtedly exists between what President Allende and the United States copper corporations regard as

[1]At the rate of progress in agrarian reform over the last decade, it would take 1000 years to complete the land redistribution.

"fair". It will be an exercise in political judgment to offer sufficient compensation to avoid the cut-off of the developmental capital Chile still needs and yet not too much to avoid alienating political support at home. The most encouraging aspect is the absence of the crisis atmosphere which so characterised similar events in Cuba a decade ago.

In Central America, great efforts were made in 1971 to repair the almost mortal damage inflicted upon the CACM by the 1969 Honduran-El Salvador war and its aftermath. All five republics realise, in varying degrees, the advantages already received by the existence of the Common Market, and that the opportunities of overcoming their underdevelopment are much greater within CACM than "going it alone". The salvage process, however, continually runs on the rocks of short-term political considerations, the hostility of El Salvador and Honduras and the lack of enthusiasm of Costa Rica which has a land frontier with only one of the four CACM group. The mood is one of pessimism derived not only from these difficulties but from the inadequacies of leaders, finance and the political will to tackle the basic problems of land reform, education and the provision of social services, which become more acute year by year, with the region's annual population growth averaging $3\frac{1}{2}$ per cent.

It is more encouraging to conclude this summary cross-section of contemporary events with the persistent optimism of Mexico's future. A new dynamic president, Echeverría, has initiated new-look economic policies designed to raise the internal spending power of the Mexican home market,[1] and to maintain the high rate of economic growth typical of recent years. Other reforms to strengthen the *ejido*, the basic unit of Mexican agrarian policy, to make the administrative machine more efficient and generally to renew the revolution indicate a more enlightened presidency than that of his predecessor, who was largely the captive of right-wing forces within the PRI.

These forces continue to prove a threat also to Echeverría, and at mid-year 1971 the issue of where to devote his efforts was still in doubt—whether to political containment of this opposition to his more populist policies or to the important social and economic measures needed to provide adequately for Mexico's mushrooming numbers.

There are two significant conclusions that may be drawn from the Mexican scene, but their relevance is much wider than their

[1]The 1970 census revealed that 5 million Mexicans, with 15 million dependents earn the equivalent of less than 36 Australian dollars a month.

application to one country. The first is that no matter how great the social transformation effected by revolutionary processes, it can be supported only by economic achievement. On such a base can also be built political strength. For over half a century these have been the foundations of Mexican stability and progress.

On the other hand, as with Uruguay, events in Mexico are an indication that no country can bask in the sunshine of its achievements. There is the constant need to adapt progress to a continuously changing world. In other words, Mexico's "adelante y arriba" is a watchword which must be the beacon for all Latin America for the years ahead.

Appendix

SOME LATIN AMERICAN PERSONALITIES

ALESSANDRI (JORGE): President of Chile 1958-64, son of one of Chile's most famous presidents, Arturo Alessandri. Wealthy industrialist, on right of political spectrum. Unsuccessfully ran against Allende in presidential election in 1970.

ALLENDE: First socialist president of Chile; elected 1970 for six year term. Doctor of medicine, previously senator since 1945, then President of the Senate. Presidential candidate 1952, 1958, 1964. Leader of FRAP (q.v.). Nationalised United States copper mines in Chile, 1971.

BANZER: President of Bolivia since August 1971; overthrew Tórrez government and its People's Assembly by military coup. Secured cooperation of ex-President Paz Estenssoro in strange coalition with former Barrientos (q.v.) supporters.

BARRIENTOS: President of Bolivia 1964-70, displacing Paz Estenssoro (q.v.). A popular army leader who claimed his government restored the Bolivian Revolution which had been "diverted from its original aims". He faced increasing opposition from the miners, and was killed in an air crash, which many consider was not accidental.

BATISTA: Effective ruler of Cuba from 1935 until his overthrow by Fidel Castro in 1959. A mulatto who as president, and as the power behind other presidents, became increasingly repressive.

BELAÚNDE: President of Peru 1963-68, democratically elected, and initiator of agrarian reform, the Amazon marginal highway and a community programme to improve the lot of the Sierra Indians. Overthrown by a military coup.

BETANCOURT: First democratic president of Venezuela, 1948, leader of Acción Democratica (q.v.). Returned to power (1958-63) after overthrow of Pérez Jiménez dictatorship. Spent twenty-one years of his life as a political prisoner. Effectively brought Venezuela into mainstream of Latin American social welfare, industrialisation and educational and agrarian reform.

BORDABERRY: President of Uruguay, elected November 1971 by very narrow majority, installed March 1972. Colorado successor to Pacheco; faces strong opposition in Congress, the problem of the Tupumaros and a sagging economy.

CALDERA: Third democratic president of Venezuela (since 1968), and leader of the Christian Democratic party (COPEI, q.v.). Most influential Latin American personality of Christian Democratic movement after Frei of Chile. A political prisoner under previous Venezuelan dictatorships.

CÁRDENAS: Mexico's greatest post-revolutionary president (1934-40); his period of office, characterised by his great personal popularity and his honest administration, saw the implementation of many social reforms, the distribution of 45 million acres of land into ejidos and the expropriation of foreign investment in Mexican oil.

CASTRO: Ruler of Cuba since 1959. By means of guerilla attacks beginning in the Sierra Maestra of eastern Cuba and increasing popular support, he overthrew the Batista dictatorship. Castro became increasingly involved in confrontation with the United States over the expropriation of the sugar interests of Cuba's neighbour. A United States sponsored invasion at the Bay of Pigs was repulsed by Castro's forces. Later Cuba's involvement with Russia led to the missile crisis of 1962.

CHÉ GUEVARA: An Argentinian revolutionary leader and collaborator with Fidel Castro of Cuba. Author of a book on the tactics of guerilla warfare, he led a revolt in eastern Bolivia where he was killed by a CIA-trained Bolivian counter-insurgency unit, in 1969.

CORTÉS: The conqueror of Mexico, 1519-20, who became the first viceroy of New Spain, which included the mainland and island territories of all Middle America.

CUAUHTÉMOC: A leader of the Aztecs whose attack on the Spanish led to their retreat from Mexico City on *La Noche Triste* (the sad night). In August, 1521, the Spaniards under Cortés attacked again, and, in spite, of a courageous resistance by his forces, Cuauhtémoc was made a prisoner.

DUVALIER: Dictator of Haiti from 1957 to his death in 1971. Elected as a progressive reformer, he became an increasingly repressive despot supported by a secret police force the *Tonton Macoutes*. He secured lavish military and economic aid from the Eisenhower administration, but Kennedy endeavoured to overthrow Duvalier by all means short of invasion.

ECHEVERRÍA: President of Mexico since 1970, lawyer, university professor and public administrator, who has re-emphasised the objectives of the Mexican social revolution, particularly in respect of its rural programme.

FREI: First Christian Democrat president of Chile, 1964-70, and leader of largest party in Chilean Congress. Secured "Chileanisation" of large American copper mines, and inaugurated important agrarian reform measures.

GAITÁN: The dynamic leader of the Colombian Liberals who in 1948 was assassinated in Bogotá. There followed three days of terror known as the *bogotazo*, and from this developed the *violencia*, an undeclared civil war throughout Colombia which probably cost the lives of a quarter of a million people over a period of some twenty years.

HAYA DE LA TORRE: The founder and leader of the *Apra* (q.v.) movement in Peru, a socialist philosophy to incorporate the Amerinds into the Peruvian nation. On several occasions the chosen president by the majority of the electorate, but consistently prevented by the armed forces from assuming office. In recent years he has collaborated with his previous opponents and thereby lost much support and influence.

HELDER CÁMARA: Archbishop of Pernambuco, one of the highest-ranking churchmen in Latin America, and the most outspoken in condemnation of the continent's social ills and of Brazil's military dictatorship. Born in the northern state of Ceará, he has identified himself with the grave economic problems of that depressed region of Brazil.

JAGAN: Leader of Guyana's People's Progressive party and elected head of the Government in 1950s and 1960s until a proportional representation constitution was arranged to prevent the continuance of his government. Supported largely by East Indian population, and clearly *persona non grata* to the United States government.

KUBITSCHEK: President of Brazil, 1951-61. Doctor of medicine, of Czechoslovak stock. Dynamic social democratic leader who established Brasilia as new capital. Deprived of civil rights in 1964 for ten years by military dictatorship.

LANUSSE: President of Argentina since March 1971 by military coup. His policies are designed to secure the incorporation of the various nationalist and Peronist groups into a political system enabling the restoration of a democratic regime in 1973, and a halt to galloping inflation.

LECHIN: The leader of the Bolivian tin miners, who has exerted a fundamental influence on political developments since the 1952 Revolution. The withdrawal of Lechin's support of the MNR triggered off the overthrow of Paz Estenssoro. Elected President of the Bolivian People's Assembly, 1971.

MÉDICI: Head of the military government of Brazil, committed to economic nationalism and policies of developmental expansion irrespective of democratic institutions and criticism.

OROZCO: A Mexican painter (1883-1949) of the revolutionary renaissance. Illustrating the struggles of peasants, workers and soldiers for emancipation he achieved dramatic effects by distortion, which grew out of his original work in social caricature.

OVANDO: Commander-In-Chief of the Bolivian army under Barrientos (q.v.), and after the death of Barrientos, for a short period, President of Bolivia.

PAZ ESTENSSORO: First president of Bolivia (1952-64) following the social revolution of 1952. Leader of the MNR (q.v.). Instituted universal suffrage, nationalised the tin mines and carried through agrarian reform measures.

PÉREZ JIMÉNEZ: Last of the Venezuelan military dictators, 1948-58: suppressed brutally all political opposition; spent lavish sums on roads and buildings particularly in Carácas. First deposed head of state ever to be extradited from the United States and returned to Venezuela in 1965 for trial.

PERÓN: Ruler of Argentina 1946-55. Since 1955 an exile in Spain. The hero of the *descamisados* (q.v.) or working class, and his social reform policies still inspire *peronista* parties in Argentina. Armed forces' opposition to *peronismo* has maintained dictatorship in Argentina since 1966.

PREBISCH: An Argentinian economic planner who was largely responsible for the creation of LAFTA. His name has been linked with the case for industrialisation as a means of increasing the standard of living, and the policy needs to sustain industrial development.

RIVERA: A Mexican painter, 1886-1957, of the revolutionary renaissance, who specialised in Mexican historical art. His masterpieces are the murals in the National Palace, and the mosaics and stone reliefs for the University City in the national capital.

SIQUEIROS: A Mexican mural painter, born in 1896, renowned for his innovations and experiments in mural painting which adorn many public buildings in Mexico City.

SOMOZA: The Somoza family, father and two sons, has maintained dictatorial control of Nicaragua since 1935. By various electoral devices and the use of puppet presidents, effective power has remained with the Somozas.

STROESSNER: Dictator of Paraguay since 1954, old-fashioned military despot whose policies are devised to maintain "stability, law and order". Opposed strongly by Catholic hierarchy since 1969.

TÓRREZ: President of Bolivia since 1970, who in 1971 sanctioned creation of a People's Assembly to assist in the government of the country. He has secured widespread support by furthering policies of Bolivia's social revolution, including nationalisation of remaining mineral enterprises. Overthrown and replaced by President Hugo Banzer in August 1971.

TRUJILLO: Dictator of the Dominican Republic from 1930 until his assassination in 1961. An opportunistic despot who repressed all opposition, maintained a national neurosis against Haiti, and organised in 1960 a plot to overthrow President Betancourt of Venezuela. Trujillo amassed a large private fortune, much of it derived from corruption in a massive programme of public works.

VELASCO ALVARADO: Leader of the left-wing military government of Peru, since 1968. The strong nationalist and social-oriented policies initiated by the military junta headed by Velasco have been dubbed *peruanismo*.

Bibliography

GENERAL

Arévalo, J. J. *The Shark and the Sardines*. Stuart, New York, 1961.

Bank of London and South America. *Review*. London, monthly.

Barclays' Bank D.C.O. *Economic Surveys*. London.

Benham, F. and Holley, H. D. *A Short Introduction to the Economy of Latin America*. Oxford University Press, London, 1960.

Bernis, S. F. *The Latin American Policy of the United States. An Historical Interpretation*. New York, 1943.

Bishop, J. *Latin America and Revolution*. Sheed & Ward, London and Melbourne, 1965.

Blakemore, H. and Smith, C. T. (ed.) *Latin America: Geographical Perspectives*. Methuen, London, 1971.

Bourne, R. *Political Leaders of Latin America*. Penguin, London, 1969.

Butland, G. J. *Latin America: A Regional Geography*. Longman, London, 1972.

Davies, H. (ed.) *The South American Handbook*. Trade & Travel Publications, Bath, annually.

Ferguson, J. H. *The Revolutions of Latin America*. Thames & Hudson, London, 1963.

Gunther, J. *Inside South America*. Hamilton, London, 1967.

Humphreys, R. A. *The Evolution of Modern Latin America*. Clarendon Press, Oxford, 1946.

Lowenthal, D. (ed.). *The West Indies Federation*. Oxford University Press, London, 1961.

Pendle, G. *A History of Latin America*. Pelican, London, 1963.

Phelps, G. *Latin America*. B.B.C., London, 1965.

Pohl, I., Zepp, J., and Webb, K. E. (ed.). *Latin America. A Geographical Commentary*. Murray, London, 1966.

Roberts, C. P. and Karplus, T. K. *Statistical Abstract of Latin America*. U.C.L.A., Los Angeles, annually.

Schneider, R. M. and Kingsbury, R. C. *An Atlas of Latin American Affairs*. Methuen, London, 1966.

Schurz, W. L. *This New World*. Allen & Unwin, London, 1956.

Thomas, A. B. *Latin America: A History*. Macmillan, New York, 1956.

Toynbee, A. J. *Between Maule and Amazon*. Oxford University Press, New York and Toronto, 1967.

Véliz, Claudio (ed.). *Latin America and the Caribbean: A Handbook*. Blond, London, 1968.

Véliz, Claudio (ed.). *Obstacles to Change in Latin America*. Oxford University Press, London, 1965.

Véliz, Claudio (ed.). *The Politics of Conformity in Latin America*. Oxford University Press, London, 1967.

West Indies and Caribbean Year Book. Skinner, London, annually.

INDIVIDUAL COUNTRIES

Chatham House studies of the Republics of Latin America. Oxford University Press for Royal Institute of International Affairs.

Butland, G. J.	*Chile* 1956.
Camacho, J. A.	*Brazil* 1954.
Cline, H. F.	*Mexico* 1962.
Galbraith, W. O.	*Colombia* 1953.
Lieuwen, E.	*Venezuela* 1961.
Linke, L.	*Ecuador* 1960.
Owens, R. J.	*Peru* 1963.
Parker, F. D.	*Central American Republics* 1963.
Pendle, G.	*Argentina* 1963; *Paraguay* 1966; *Uruguay* 1963.
Smith, R. T.	*British Guiana* 1962.

Alexander, R. J. *The Perón Era*. Gollancz, London, 1957.

Alexander, R. J. *The Bolivian National Revolution*. Rutgers, New Bruns., 1958.

Blanksten, G. I. *Perón's Argentina*. Cambridge University Press, London, 1953.

Butland, G. J. "Latin American Dilemma" *World Review*. Vol. 4, No. 1. Jacaranda, Brisbane, March 1965.

Carey, J. C. *Peru and the United States. 1900-62*. University of Notre Dame Press, 1964.

Fitzgibbon, R. H. *Uruguay: Portrait of a Democracy*. Allen & Unwin, London, 1956.

Freyre, G. *The Masters and the Slaves*. Knopf, New York, 1946.

Gil, F. G. *The Political System of Chile*. Houghton Mifflin, Boston, 1966.

Goldenberg, B. *The Cuban Revolution and Latin America*. London, 1965.

Gross, L. *The Last, Best Hope: Eduardo Frei and Chilean Democracy*. New York, 1967.

Hanson, E. P. *Puerto Rico: Ally for Progress*. Van Nostrand, Princeton, 1962.

Kalijarvi, T. V. *Central America. Land of Lords and Lizards*. Van Nostrand, New York, 1962.

Meneses, E. *Fidel Castro*. Faber, London, 1968.

Owen, F. *Perón. His Rise and Fall*. The Cresset Press, London, 1957.

Scheer, R. and Zeitlin, M. *Cuba: an American Tragedy*. Penguin, London, 1964.

Spender, S. and Lasky, M. J. (ed.). *Rediscovering Latin America—Encounter*. Vol. XXV, No. 3. London, Sept. 1965.

Wagley, C. *Amazon Town: a Study of Man in the Tropics*. Macmillan, New York, 1952.

Wagley, C. *et al. Race and Class in Rural Brazil*. UNESCO, Paris, 1952.

JOURNALS

American Geographical Society

Focus articles on
Bahamas, Dominican Republic, Haiti, Jamaica, Mexico, Puerto Rico, Bolivia, Brazil, Buenos Aires, Colombia, Ecuador, Guyana, Paraguay and Peru. 1963-69.

Latin American Research Review. University of Texas Press.

Blasier, Cole. *Studies of Social Revolution: Origins in Mexico, Bolivia and Cuba*. pp. 28-64.

Mangin, William. *Latin American Squatter Settlements: A Problem and a Solution*. pp. 65-98.

McAlister, L. N. *Recent Research and Writings on the Role of the Military in Latin America*. Vol. II, No. 3, 1967, pp. 5-36.

Morse, Richard M. *Recent Research on Latin American Urbanisation. A Selective Survey with Commentary*. Vol. 1, No. 1, 1965, pp. 35-74.

Schaedel, Richard P. *Land Reform Studies*. Vol. 1, No. 2, 1966, pp. 75-122.

Wolfe, Marshall. *Rural Settlement Patterns and Social Change in Latin America: Notes for a Strategy of Rural Development*. Vol. II, No. 1, 1966. pp. 5-50.

Glossary

Acción Popular: the Popular Action party of President Belaúnde against perennial dictatorship: assumed its present title in 1941: secured the election of Dr Rómulo Betancourt and Dr Raúl Leoni as Presidents of Venezuela in 1959 and 1964 respectively.

Acción Popular: the Popular Action party of President Belaúnde of Peru, founded in 1956.

Amerind: American Indian, the indigenous inhabitant of the Americas.

Apra: Alianza Popular Revolucionaria Americana, the American Popular Revolutionary party of Haya de la Torre (Peru); members of the party known as *Apristas*, the philosophy as *Aprismo*.

Asamblea del Pueblo: the Assembly of the People, the parliament created by President Tórrez of Bolivia in 1971.

Aymará and Quechua: the principal Indian languages of Bolivia and Peru. Some 70 per cent of Bolivians are either Aymará or Quechua speaking.

Aztecs: the final pre-Conquest Indian cultural group who controlled Central Mexico. A warrior tribe who imposed their rule on the higher Toltec culture, and began an orgy of human sacrifice to avert disaster and maintain the sun in the heavens.

barriada: an urban fringe settlement, usually of sub-standard housing.

Blancos and Colorados: the major political parties of Uruguay for over a century, derived from opposing factions in the nineteenth century who wore white (blanco) or red (colorado) as their distinguishing colours. Traditionally the Colorados are liberal and the Blancos conservative in political philosophy. The tensions arising from the Tupumoras' (q.v.) opposition to President Pacheco's government in 1971 appear to be leading to a complete fragmentation of both Blancos and Colorados and a re-alignment of new political parties.

caatinga: semi-arid vegetation, particularly characteristic of North-east Brazil.

CACM.: Central American Common Market.

cafuso: Indian-Negro racial mixture (Brazil).

callampa: literally "mushroom", the shack dwellings which spring up overnight to house migrants on the urban fringes.

campo cerrado: savanna (tropical grassland) with many trees (Brazil).

campo limpo: savanna (tropical grassland) largely treeless (Brazil).

Carifta: Caribbean Free Trade Association.

carretera marginal de la selva: marginal highway of the jungle (Peru), a major project initiated by President Belaúnde.

caudillo: the military junta leader.

ceja de montaña: mountain borderland of eastern Andes of Peru, literally "the eyebrow of the jungle".

Companhia de Melhoramentos Norte do Paraná: Northern Paraná Improvement Company, sponsoring development and settlement of northern Paraná (Brazil).

conquistador: the colonial conquest leader who subdued Indian resistance.

Cooperación Popular: a programme of voluntary aid to help Indian communities towards modernisation, initiated by President Belaúnde of Peru: a form of "Peace Corps".

COPEI: the Committee for Independent Political and Electoral Organisation, the Venezuelan Social Christian party (Christian Democratic), established in 1946, and the support of President Rafael Caldera.

costa: coastal zone.

descamisados: literally "the shirtless ones", the under-privileged social groups, for whom President Perón of Argentina devised his social welfare legislation.

dystrophy: faulty nutrition.

ejido: community farm resulting from agrarian reform in Mexico.

favela: fringe settlement of sub-standard dwellings (Brazil).

FRAP: Frente de Acción Popular, the Popular Front of Socialist and Communist parties, supporting President Salvador Allende of Chile, elected 1970.

hacienda: large, self-contained farm-estate, usually a legacy of the colonial past.

haciendados: the owners and social class of the *hacienda* proprietorship.

Indo-America: a term stressing the basic Amerind cultural and ethnic component of "Latin" America.

LAFTA: Latin American Free Trade Association.

latifundia: system of large farm-estates, with associated sociological framework.

marcha para o oueste: the drive to the west, the interior colonisation of Brazil.

meseta: high tableland surface.

mestizo: European-Indian racial mixture.

minifundia: system of fragmented agricultural holdings, frequently of uneconomic size and potential.

MNR: the Movimiento Nacionalista Revolucionario, the Revolutionary Nationalist Party of Bolivia, formed in 1941, by Paz Estenssoro, and based on an alliance between the nationalist middle classes and organised labour. The motive force behind the Bolivian social revolution.

mulatto: European-Negro racial mixture.

occupance: a geographical term indicating the process of occupying or living in an area and the transformations of the original landscape which result.

Peronismo: the political philosophy and policies of President Perón of Argentina, 1946-55.

Peruanismo: the left-wing, nationalist philosophy of the military regime of President Velasco of Peru, 1970-71.

physiography: a term used to include all the aspects of the natural landscape, structure, relief, climatic characteristics, vegetation etc.

Platt Amendment: the provision by which the United States was given the right to intervene in Cuba's affairs and thus to transform the island into a virtual protectorate. Enacted in 1901, it was abrogated in 1934 by Franklin Roosevelt.

PRI: Partido Revolucionario Institutional. The Institutional Revolutionary party of Mexico representing the corporate interests supporting the Mexican social revolution: assumed its present title in 1946.

sertão: isolated, little-known area, remote from populated centres (Brazil); almost equivalent to the Australian "bush".

sierra: mountain range.

Tierra y Libertad: Land and Liberty, the slogan of the Mexican social revolution, emphasising the vital function of land reform in the emancipation of the Mexican people.

Tupumaros: urban guerillas of Montevideo (Uruguay) opposing the Government in 1970-71. They derive their name from José Gabriel Tupac-Amaru and his brother who, in Peru and Bolivia, headed the first great war of independence, 1781.

villa miseria: literally "misery suburb", shack housing of urban fringe squatters.

violencia: literally "the violence", referring to the civil war which raged for many years in many parts of Colombia after the assassination of Gaitán in 1948.

zambo: Indian-Negro racial mixture (Brazil).

Index